HOUSE POOR

HOUSE
POOR

How to Buy and Sell Your Home

Come Bubble or Bust

June Fletcher

Collins

An Imprint of HarperCollinsPublishers

This book is written as a source of information only. The information contained in this book should by no means be considered a substitute for the advice, decisions, or judgment of the reader's legal, tax, financial, or other professional advisor.

All efforts have been made to ensure the accuracy of the information contained in this book as of the date published. The author and the publisher expressly disclaim responsibility for any adverse effects arising from the use of the application of the information contained herein.

HarperCollins books may be purchased for educational, business, or sales promotional use. For information please write: Special Markets Department, HarperCollins Publishers, 10 East 53rd Street, New York, NY 10022.

FIRST COLLINS PAPERBACK EDITION PUBLISHED 2006

Designed by Jaime Putorti

The Library of Congress has catalogued the hardcover edition as follows:

Library of Congress Cataloging-in-Publication Data

Fletcher, June, 1951–
  House poor: pumped up prices, rising rates, and mortgages on steroids : how to survive the coming housing crisis / by June Fletcher.
    p. cm.
Includes bibliographical references and index.
ISBN-13: 978-0-06-087322-6
ISBN-10: 0-06-087322-1
  1. Residential real estate—United States. 2. Housing—Prices—United States. 3. Home ownership—United States. 4. Mortgage loans—United States. 5. Interest rates—United States. 6. Inflation (Finance)—United States. I. Title.

HD259.F58 2006
33.33'23'0973—dc23   2005051998

ISBN-10: 0-06-087323-X (pbk.)
ISBN-13: 978-0-06-087323-3 (pbk.)

06 07 08 09 10 ❖/RRD 10 9 8 7 6 5 4 3 2 1

To David and Adam, with love

CONTENTS

PREFACE

Some books are based on years of scholarship and study; some on breaking news—this book falls into the latter category.

Although rumblings of a housing bubble have been heard since the tech bubble exploded in 2000, it all seemed like distant thunder until the spring and summer of 2005. That's when numerous industry insiders began to express serious concerns about double-digit home price increases, the proliferation of risky loans, and the explosion of real estate speculators. It all seemed eerily familiar, not just reminiscent of the tech bubble, but of speculative manias in the past. Nearly every media outlet in the country jumped on the story, with a similar message: The hot market is about to turn cold—beware.

Yes, but then what? That's what I took as the starting point of this book, which was written during the crescendo of media attention on the subject. It's now pretty clear that the real estate boom is over. It's time to move from a speculative to a more sober attitude about our homes.

Having invested so much in our homes, it's scary for most of us to think about what is going to happen now that the market has turned. I hope what I've learned from more than two decades of real estate reporting, through several boom and bust cycles, will help you to survive, and even thrive, in the shifting economics of a postbubble world.

ACKNOWLEDGMENTS

Portions of this book have been adapted from articles that I have written for the *Wall Street Journal* and from columns that I have done for RealEstateJournal.com

My thanks to the Collins publishing team for their wisdom and encouragement as this book was quickly brought to fruition, especially editor Herb Schaffner, copy chief Diane Aronson, assistant Alexandra Kaufman, and copyeditor David Falk.

I'm also indebted to super-agent Howard Yoon of the Gail Ross Literary Agency for introducing me to HarperCollins, and for his savvy and resourcefulness.

I'd like to thank the *Wall Street Journal* for giving me the time to do this book, especially vice president of news operations Jim Penserio and editors Joanne Lipman, Ed Felsenthal, Amy Stevens, Jeff Grocott, and Sam Grobart, as well as RealEstateJournal.com's Laura Lorber, Valerie Patterson, and Lauren Kim. My appreciation also goes to my Dow Jones colleagues and friends who gave me advice, assistance, and leads, especially Ken Wells, Carrie Dolan, Alexandra Peers, Danielle Reed, Nancy Keates, Troy McMullen, Amir Efrati, Kristen Carr, Steve Barnes, Barbara Scott, and Virginia Cahill.

No book on home prices could have been done without the insights of many housing economists. For helping to further my understanding, I'd particularly like to thank David Stiff, Robert Shiller, and Karl Case of FISERV/CSW; John Tuccillo of JTA, Inc.; Frank Nothaft of Freddie Mac; Dave Seiders and Gopal Ahluwalia of the National Association of Home Builders; Doug Duncan of the Mortgage Bankers Association, and David Lereah and Lawrence Yun of the National Association of Realtors.

For their 24/7 support, guidance, and understanding, I'm also grateful to my long-time friends Ann Marie Moriarty, Brad German, and William Young. My friends in the National Association of Real Estate Editors and the Carpers Farm Book Club also provided support and smart advice.

I also want to thank my wise and patient family, including my brother Gary Fletcher, my in-laws, Sid and Edna Silverberg, and my brother-in-law Paul Silverberg, his wife, Nancy, and their children. (Now maybe we can visit.) And finally, my love and endless gratitude goes to this book's first readers, my husband, David Silverberg, and son Adam Fletcher Silverberg. While I stayed up late writing about houses, they took care of ours.

A Wild Ride

Anyone who has gambled in the housing market over the past few years has been on a roller-coaster ride. One year, you're fending off buyers clamoring to snatch up their homes in bidding wars; the next, you're slashing prices, repainting the bathrooms, and throwing in the Lexus just to get someone—anyone—to show up at your open house.

So if you're feeling queasy these days, I don't blame you. Housing, like any other investment, has always had its ups and downs. But ever since it started its upswing at the beginning of this decade, the ride has become more thrilling—and also more dangerous. That's when professional investors, soured on equities, began to snatch up beach houses instead of cyberstocks, shrinking supply and pushing up home prices. Seeing the fortunes that were being made flipping real estate, and watching mortgage interest rates fall, soon everyone wanted to hop aboard. Annual double-digit price growth became common in major coastal cities across America. From 2000 to 2005, some places, like Los Angeles and Miami, saw price gains of more than 150 percent.

The Double-Digit Club

From 2000 to 2005, many places throughout the country saw double-digit average annual price gains. Here are 10 in different states, compiled by Cambridge, Massachusetts, research company FISERV/CSW:

Place/Zip	Median Home Price	5-Year Appreciation
Glendale, CA 91203	$440,000	174%
Brigantine, NJ 08203	$350,000	146.9%
Miami, FL 33138	$340,000	136.4%
Manorville, NY 11949	$440,000	128%
Warren, RI 02885	$275,000	127.6%
Marion, MA 02738	$550,000	112.6%
Boulder City, NV 89005	$293,500	109.5%
Silver Spring, MD 20910	$399,000	106.4%
St. Paul, MN 55108	$228,000	83.6%
Hollis, NH 03049	$350,000	82.5%

But now as I write this, in the summer of 2006, housing has passed its peak—and in some places, has already begun what could be a dizzying drop. Across the country, sales have slowed and supply is building up. (In fact, there are almost four million homes available for sale nationwide, and inventories are at record high levels.). Houses that used to sell in two days are lingering on the market for two months or longer. Nationally, homes are still appreciating, but the rate of price growth has slowed significantly, from 13.4 percent in the fourth quarter of 2005 to 9.5 percent in the first quarter of 2006. Some of the toniest and most expensive places in America, including Palm Springs, California, and Palm Beach, Florida, are showing slight price declines. It won't be long, I think, before homeowners in other places start to feel the competitive pressure, and cut their prices, too.

None of this is surprising, really. Pundits have been predicting the cooling of the superheated housing market for more than a year. So have many alert would-be buyers, like Seattle newlyweds John and Becky Mayer. They sat out the housing boom in a cramped one-bedroom apartment because they were worried that the dot-com debacle of the late '90s would be repeated soon in real estate. "There's only one way for this trend to go, and that's straight down," says Mr. Mayer.

The Mayers are probably right, because rampant speculation is a big reason that the housing market got overblown in the first place. In 2005, nearly a fourth of all homes were bought as investments, about four times the number found in less overheated times, according to the National Association of Realtors. Many were novices to real estate investing who were taking advantage of historically low interest rates: folks like 31-year-old Lori Kim, who was able to buy a house and two condos in Las Vegas during the height of the boom, primarily using home-equity loans.

But the low interest rates that fueled speculation—and also allowed seven out of 10 Americans to own their own homes—are now inching up. In 2003 a fixed rate, 30-year mortgage could be had for 5.28 percent; at this writing, the average rate is 6.78 percent. According to the National Association of Realtors, in 2005, homeowners were paying an average of 24% more in principal and interest payments than they were just two years earlier: $1,040 a month, compared to $840. And that's not counting other monthly expenses that have risen over the past couple of years, like property taxes (a by-product of rising home prices) and energy costs.

Add stagnating salaries and a taste for high-ticket toys like plasma televisions to the picture, and you can see why attitudes and housing markets have changed so suddenly. People are no longer worried about making it rich as flippers; they're worried about keeping a roof over their heads. The Joint Center for Housing Studies at Harvard University says about a quarter of middle-class homeowners, 9.3. million in all, are overextending themselves on housing.

A Northern Virginia real estate agent I know has been caught in the shifting currents. In the fall of 2005, he took out a large home-equity loan to buy an investment home for his college-bound son, planning to sell it quickly and use the profits to pay for his son's tuition. But now, six months later, prices in his market have softened so much, he can't even sell the home for what he'd paid for it—and meanwhile, the interest rate on his home-equity loan continues to tick up. "I stay awake at night worrying and wondering what to do," he says.

Rising mortgage rates also are troubling for homeowners who stretched to buy during the boom and just squeaked by their lender's minimum requirements by taking adjustable or variable-rate loans. Although federal regulators are now cracking down on lenders who try to push these loans on people who really can't afford them, that doesn't help those who've already acquired them. And once these loans adjust upwards, as many are now doing, buyers who could just barely afford to make their initial payments will be pushed to the brink of bankruptcy.

The consequences could be disastrous. Already, foreclosures are on the rise in many cities around the country: in April 2006, they were up 15 percent in Dallas from six months earlier, while in Minneapolis they were up 43 percent. Though national foreclosure rates remain low, experts worry that this state of affairs won't last long once rates rise further and already-stretched budgets reach the breaking point. Risky lending practices could create a reprisal of the early '90s, when lenders suddenly found themselves flooded with foreclosed homes. Contrary to stereotype, not all of these foreclosed homes are in the slums; some are in the very best neighborhoods. For instance, one recent foreclosure listing was for a lakefront home with five bedrooms and six baths in toney Lake Oswego, Oregon. Price tag: $3.8 million.

All of this is bad news for sellers, but what about buyers? Aren't they the winners in this otherwise depressing scenario? Can't they gain from sellers' pain?

Not necessarily. Lenders have long figured that a family can afford to spend 28% of its gross monthly income on housing expenses. But prices have risen so high and so fast over the last few years, they've outstripped incomes in every major city in America, especially on the coasts. In some, according to an index published jointly by the National Association of Home Builders and Wells Fargo, the percentage of homes that are affordable to median-income households is alarmingly low. By their measure, only 8% of homes are affordable for San Francisco residents, and 6% for New Yorkers. In Los Angeles, the percentage is only 2%. Unless prices fall dramatically in these and other important cities—and interest rates remain low—would-be buyers will remain on the sidelines.

How Affordable?

Although homes in the Midwest generally remain affordable for buyers making the median income, that's not true in many other places. Below is a sampling of cities showing the share of homes that could be afforded by buyers making the area's median income in the first quarter of 2006, as compiled by the National Association of Home Builders and Wells Fargo.

St. Louis, MO	83.1%
Denver-Aurora, CO	62.4%
Austin-Round Rock, TX	58.3%
Salt Lake City, UT	50.1%
Baltimore-Towson, MD	49.1%
Honolulu, HA	34.4%
Seattle-Bellevue-Everett, WA	32.6%
Las Vegas-Paradise, NV	19.4%
Miami-Miami Beach-Kendall, FL	13.6%
San Diego-Carlsbad-San Marcos, CA	5.2%

So how will this stomach-churning ride end? Some experts, like Dean Baker, codirector of the Center for Economic and Policy Research in Washington, D.C., says many buyers who bought when prices were near or at their peak will see "substantial losses" once the market tumbles. Others say a whoopee cushion is a better metaphor for how the overall market is likely to behave. "The air will escape, but slowly," says Cambridge economist David Stiff.

In the near future, resort areas like Las Vegas and Miami, both favorites of investors, will probably be most vulnerable to price declines. But, really, anywhere is vulnerable if a military base or major local employer closes, jobs are suddenly out-sourced overseas, or there's some unanticipated disaster, like an act of terrorism or a chemical plant spill. "You just don't know when the next economic shock will happen," says Frank Nothaft, chief economist for Freddie Mac. "That's when bad things happen to good people."

FROM BOOM TO BUST—AND BACK AGAIN

As exhilarating as the ride up to the peak of the housing cycle has been for home owners—and as frightening as the ride down looks—such manias have happened before. In his classic book, *Financial Euphoria*, economist John Kenneth Galbraith outlines the stages they all follow. First, something new and desirable is identified, like tulips in Holland, and the price goes up. This attracts new buyers, and the pace of steps up to panic buying levels. During this wave of speculation, two types of buyers emerge: those that think the prices will go up indefinitely, and those who expect it to end, but think they're smart enough to get out before the market crashes.

And crash it always does, when something—"it matters little," he says—spooks investors into taking their profits, creating a rush for the exits. "And thus the rule, supported by the experience of centuries: the speculative episode always ends not with a whimper, but with a bang."

While everyone knows you should buy low and sell high, it's difficult to avoid the herd mentality. Certainly that's been true for stock market investors. In November 1999, two months before the tech bubble burst, the UBS/Gallup Index of Investor Optimism hit the highest confidence level ever recorded. The index's lowest point? In March 2003, right as the S&P 500 started a year-long climb of more than 40%.

Real estate investors have been no different. In the summer of 2005, just when housing prices were peaking, a quarter of Americans said it was a good time to buy because prices were to rise—the highest percentage since 1988, when prices last peaked. Tom Faber, author of *Tomorrow's Gold*, another book on investment manias, writes that it's not unusual to see even sophisticated investors buying in the late stages of a bubble, because that's when prices spike most dramatically and "profit opportunities with leveraged positions are vast."

In retrospect, the panicked attempts to buy anything with four walls in the months leading up to last summer's peak seem sadly misguided. In Manhattan, bidding wars were so fierce that one buyer spent $250,000 over the $1.35 million asking price to snare a modest two-bedroom apartment. In Bonita Bay, a master-planned community in Southwest Florida, buyers paid $50,000 to hold a spot on a waiting list to buy a condo costing upwards of $620,000 in a new high-rise. Lake Las Vegas, Nevada, Woodside Homes were so beset by speculators that they required buyers to sign a deed restriction that prevents selling, leasing, or timesharing a home for a year after purchase. (Only disability, severe illness, job transfer, or death could void the rule.) Violators could be charged $50,000.

Of course, some of the tremendous price increases of the housing boom were stage-managed by home builders, who set the standards for prices and control the supply. By holding campouts and lotteries for new projects, they helped whip already frothy markets into a panic.

But most home builders are too sophisticated to believe that prices will run up forever. Indeed, many began to pull back on building just when housing hit its peak, in anticipation of rising mortgage rates. They remembered the last recession in the early '90s, when housing was overbuilt after another speculative boom. Some were caught owning big tracts of land just when the stream of customers dried up.

Now, most builders are much more cautious, starting construction only when they've nailed the sale rather than building on speculation, and buying piecemeal on "rolling options" rather than purchasing complete parcels outright. In May 2006, typically a banner month for building, single-family permits were down 4% from the year before.

Still, even home builders can be caught up in a boom mentality. For instance, over the last three years, many national home builders entered the Washington, D.C., metro area for the first time, attracted by the area's high income level and seemingly "recession-proof" government-based economy. As prices rose into the double-digits, they built and built. Eventually, they overbuilt the market—and killed it in the process.

Now the *Washington Post* is filled with real estate ads from builders offering buyers triple closing costs, $500 gasoline cards, and three-years' paid utility bills, as well as more typical incentives like free sunrooms and finished basements. Some are even cutting prices outright, an unusual and desperate-sounding move, because it's sure to anger early buyers in their communities who paid full price.

Besides all these signs that housing is cooling, there are other ominous economic portents these days, like the flattening gap in the yield curve between long-term and short-term interest rates—traditionally an early warning sign of a recession. And the "vultures" are literally circling—vulture capitalists, that is, who create funds to buy properties cheaply when a market collapses. Experienced real estate investors are getting nervous: Oakton, Virginia, investor Nicholas Nikzad, who first started buying homes in the late '70s and early '80s, when interest rates were as high as 18%, isn't buying anything now. "Everyone's on the ledge," he says.

He's right to be worried. A 2003 study by the International Monetary Fund looked at the effects of housing market busts in the United States and 13 other industrialized countries that happens on average every two decades. They compared it to stock market crashes. They found even when a house price decline is only half as large as a stock market bust, it causes twice the damage to the economy, and the effects linger twice as long.

Why? Housing price declines have a ripple effect all through the economy, knocking out jobs in construction and banking, and hurting sales of home-related products, from roofing to rugs. As owners see their net worth fall, they spend less on other things too, no longer eating out as much or going on fancy vacations, and buying cars and clothes less frequently. Lowered spending leads to layoffs, and people without jobs don't buy houses.

So how do you cope in these uncertain times?

We're here to give you some survival tips, through expert advice and stories from real people who've ridden real estate's wild ride and emerged unscathed. For instance, you'll meet Sheri and Art Armendariz, who figured out a clever way to buy and live in their dream home on the ocean, and make others pay for it. You'll hear how Adam Brauer took advantage of low interest rates without getting over his head in debt. And you'll find out how Jeff and Laura Czaja got a toehold in one of the country's most expensive real estate markets by buying a fixer-upper and tapping their friends for sweat equity.

Riding against the Herd: The Kimballs' Story

Two decades ago, Mary Doyle Kimball and her husband Dave bought a small house in Boca Raton, Florida. "It was an ugly little house, but it was near the beach," says Ms. Kimball, the executive director for a nonprofit journalist association. After living there for five years, they moved to a nicer and bigger house nearby, but decided to keep their first house as an investment property and rent it out.

Over the years, Boca Raton's housing market got hotter and hotter, and the ugly little place near the beach became more and more valuable. Six years ago, annual property taxes had risen to about $5,000, and the Kimballs began thinking about selling. The neighborhood had grown trendy. Builders and real estate agents kept sniffing around the house, which was temporarily vacant, hoping they could buy it, tear it down and build a McMansion. Offers that were ten times what they originally paid for the house poured in.

Instead, they decided to refinance the home they lived in with an interest-only adjustable-rate loan, and use the money to pay their investment home's taxes. Going from a high fixed-rate loan at close to 10% to a low interest-only adjustable-rate loan at close to 3% lowered their monthly payments dramatically, from $1,900 to $600 a month.

Though interest-only loans subsequently became popular (for more on this, see Chapter Two), at the time, they were rare, accounting for less than 2% of all loans. Initially, the Kimballs felt nervous about taking out a mortgage that wouldn't let them build up any equity in their home. "We didn't tell the neighbors, because

(continued)

we were afraid they'd be horrified. We thought they'd think we were the grasshoppers and they were the ants."

But their gamble paid off. Prices continued to climb in Boca Raton. For the past 10 months, Ms. Kimball estimates the house has increased in value at the rate of $19,000 a month. Recently, they decided to sell for $665,000, and are looking to acquire another investment property in a tax-deferred exchange.

This time, however, they'll probably pay cash, or finance with a fixed-rate loan. They won't go with an interest-only adjustable, even though it's the rage with their neighbors and friends. Rates are on the rise, which makes it a bad time to take more financial risks than necessary. Once again, the Kimballs hope to win the real estate game by ignoring the herd mentality. "This isn't the time to mess with your nest egg," says Ms. Kimball.

My goal through these pages is to help you through all the steps you'll need to consider in a slowing market, as you decide whether it's better to rent than buy; how to avoid crushing debt and tricky lenders; how to stage, photograph, and market a home in the Internet age; how to get an edge in negotiations with real estate agents and builders; how to sell a home yourself, and how to tap into the huge pool of buyers overseas.

Finally, I'll show you how to get your bearings during dramatic housing cycles that can whipsaw both sellers and buyers. And while no one can perfectly predict when home prices will be highest or lowest, I'll give you some clues to help you figure out where they're headed. . . . so no matter which way the wild ride twists and turns, you'll never have to say you're house poor.

1

To Buy or Not to Buy, That Is the Question

April and Adam Nichols are suffering from sticker shock. The newlywed New Yorkers would love to get out of their cramped one-bedroom rental in Manhattan, which costs them $2,325 a month, and buy a starter condo. But everything they've seen in their under-$500,000 price range is horrible. One place they looked at in Hoboken, New Jersey, was a fifth-floor walk-up with a view of an ugly brick wall. Another in the Bronx was in a run-down building populated by folks fifty years their senior. And as for buying in pricey Manhattan itself—well, unless you're Donald Trump himself, fuggedaboudit.

So what are the Nicholses planning to do? For now, nothing. "It's hard to throw money away on rent, but we're going to be patient," says Ms. Nichols. "Prices are bound to come down."

It's hard to sit on the sidelines when every day, the news profiles hairdressers, truck drivers, and schoolteachers making thousands flipping properties. And it's harder still when the airwaves are crammed with home-fix-up shows, and when bookstores are filled with books on how to make millions as a real estate investor.

But to every thing there is a time and a season, and that's as true for home buying as it is for everything else. The people who win big in the real estate game are the ones with the courage to sit out the manias as markets reach their peaks and buy during the busts. As Shakespeare wrote: "Ripeness is all."

The trick is to be contrarian and recognize where you are in the real estate cycle. When Doug Duncan, chief economist for the Mortgage Bankers Association, moved to Washington, D.C., in 1988, the local real estate market was sizzling and buyers got caught up in bidding wars at open houses. He decided to rent. Soon, the market took a nosedive. Five years later, he decided it would be a good time to buy. He paid about a third less than the previous owner, who'd lost his home in a foreclosure. "You have to use caution," he says. (We'll show you how in Chapter 6.)

Understandably, not many real estate brokers share this opinion. An ad sent to clients by agents of the New York brokerage Prudential Douglas Elliman pushes ownership hard, even in today's hair-raising market. It points out that real estate prices, unlike stocks, adjust slowly, and that predictions that the New York market would crash after 9/11 didn't come to pass. It also tells first-time home buyers that they have to "get in the elevator to ride to the penthouse," and asks: "Why do you work so hard? To live in a crummy rental for the rest of your life waiting for a bargain to emerge?"

But the real worry today isn't that you'll be stuck in a rental for the rest of your life, but that you'll buy at the peak and be stuck in the property for an entire real estate cycle, which can last for years, waiting for prices to recover. To come out ahead as investors, we need to buy low and sell high, but this gets forgotten in the emotions of buying a home.

So how often do busts occur? The Federal Deposit Insurance Corporation (FDIC) has identified 21 cities that experienced a housing bust over the last quarter-century. In the mid-1980s, the victims were cities in Texas, Louisiana, Oklahoma, and other places that depended on oil prices. In the early '90s, cities in the Northeast and California, which had experienced big, unsustainable home price run-ups, were hit. Scattered throughout the country were other places that experienced price declines when they lost major employers or became overbuilt. After too many developers invaded Honolulu, for instance, the city had six straight years of price declines, ending in 2001.

Although the FDIC notes that booms don't always end in busts—often, there is simply a period of price stagnation—the agency adds that the number of boom cities increased by 72%, to 55, in 2004, mostly near the coasts. More than half of these places had never experienced a boom before.

How genuine is the danger of price declines today? Some economists like David Lereah, chief economist for the National Association of Realtors, argue that we're not in danger at all, because current long-term fundamentals are sound. In his recent book *Are You Missing the Real Estate Boom?*, Mr. Lereah points to a number of factors that he thinks will keep the boom propped up indefinitely, including healthy job growth, tight supply, and continued demand by retirees, foreigners, Baby Boomers, and their children. He predicts prices will rise 9% this year nationwide, with even greater gains in markets on the coasts. "This real estate boom has wings," he writes.

Table 1. Historical Evidence of U.S. Home Price Booms and Busts, 1978 - 2004

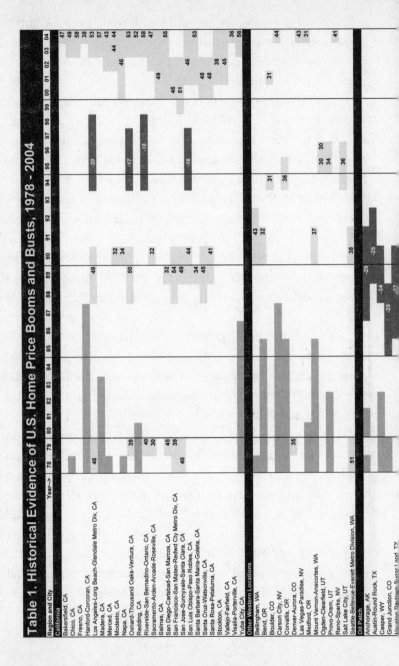

Region and City	78	79	80	81	82	83	84	85	86	87	88	89	90	91	92	93	94	95	96	97	98	99	00	01	02	03	04
California																											
Bakersfield, CA																											47
Chico, CA																											49
Fresno, CA																											58
Hanford-Corcoran, CA																											38
Los Angeles-Long Beach-Glendale Metro Div, CA	46											49						-20									53
Madera, CA																											57
Merced, CA																										44	43
Modesto, CA																									46	44	44
Napa, CA		39										50	32					-17									53
Oxnard-Thousand Oaks-Ventura, CA													34					-18									52
Redding, CA			40																								58
Riverside-San Bernadino-Ontario, CA		30																									47
Sacramento-Arden-Arcade-Roseville, CA												32	32														55
Salinas, CA																											
San Diego-Carlsbad-San Marcos, CA	45																										
San Francisco-San Mateo-Redwd Cty Metro Div, CA		39																									
San Jose-Sunnyvale-Santa Clara, CA												32	44					-16									53
San Luis Obispo-Paso Robles, CA												54															
Santa Barbara-Santa Maria-Goleta, CA												49															
Santa Cruz-Watsonville, CA												34															
Santa Rosa-Petaluma, CA												45	41										46				
Stockton, CA																							51	48			
Vallejo-Fairfield, CA																								48	38		
Visalia-Porterville, CA																									45		36
Yuba City, CA	40																										56
Other Western Locations																											
Bellingham, WA																											
Bend, OR													43	32													44
Boulder, CO																	31							31			
Carson City, NV																		30	30								
Corvallis, OR																	36	34									
Denver-Aurora, CO																											43
Las Vegas-Paradise, NV		35																									31
Medford, OR														37													
Mount Vernon-Anacortes, WA																			36								
Ogden-Clearfield, UT																											
Provo-Orem, UT																											
Reno-Sparks, NV																											41
Salt Lake City, UT																											
Seattle-Bellevue-Everett Metro Division, WA	51												38														
Oil Patch																											
Anchorage, AK												-29															
Austin-Round Rock, TX													-25														
Casper, WY										-29	-34																
Grand Junction, CO																											

City			
Odessa, TX			
Oklahoma City, OK			
San Antonio, TX	−17		
New England			
Barnstable Town, MA			48
Boston-Quincy Metro Division, MA		62	38
Bridgeport-Stamford-Norwalk, CT		74	
Burlington-South Burlington, VT		71	
Hartford-West Hartford-East Hartford, CT	−17	32	35
Manchester-Nashua, NH		61	
New Haven-Milford, CT		55	
Norwich-New London, CT	−17	76	31
Portland-South Portland-Biddeford, ME	−20	50	30
Providence-New Bedford-Fall River-Warwick, RI	−16	47	46
Springfield, MA	−16	69	
Worcester, MA-CT		63 / 71	34
Other Northeast			
Albany-Schenectady-Troy, NY		49	40
Allentown-Bethlehem-Easton, PA-NJ		48	36
Atlantic City, NJ			30
Baltimore-Towson, MD			41
Hagerstown-Martinsburg, MD-WV			
Kingston, NY		67	30
New York-Wayne-White Plains Metro Division, NY			33
Ocean City, NJ			44
Philadelphia Metro Division, PA			30
Poughkeepsie-Newburgh-Middletown, NY		42	41
Scranton-Wilkes-Barre-Hazelton, PA		63	
Trenton-Ewing, NJ		31	32
Virginia Beach-Norfolk-Newport News, VA-NC			31
Washington-Arlington-Alexandria Metro Div, DC		61	40
Winchester, VA-WV		31	35
Florida			
Cape Coral-Fort Myers, FL			38
Deltona-Daytona Beach-Ormond Beach, FL			35
Fort Walton Beach-Crestview-Destin, FL			32
Miami-Miami Beach-Kendall Metro Division, FL			45
Naples-Marco Island, FL			35
Palm Bay-Melbourne-Titusville, FL			43
Panama City-Lynn Haven, FL			30
Port St. Lucie-Fort Pierce, FL			54
Punta Gorda, FL			42
Sarasota-Bradenton-Venice, FL			37
Vero Beach, FL			38
Other			
Honolulu, HI	30	60	35
Peoria, IL	−16	−16	

LEGEND:
BOOM = Years where real home prices increased at least 30 percent from 3 years earlier.
BUST = Years where nominal home prices declined from 5 years earlier.
(City must include at least one 5-year period where nominal price declined by more than 15 percent.)
Numbers in bold indicate maximum 3-year real price increase in a boom, or maximum nominal 5-year price decline in a bust; duplicate numbers in bold indicate the same maximum was reached in two separate years.
N/A = Missing price data

Source: FDIC FYI Revisited "U.S. Home Prices: Does Bust Always Follow Boom?" May 2, 2005. (Office of Federal Housing Enterprise Oversight House Price Index, nominal and real, using Bureau of Labor Statistics Consumer Price Index less shelter inflation index).

But though nominal prices haven't fallen since the 1930s, real home prices have tumbled from time to time, typically after a big run-up like we're seeing today. In the early '80s, real home prices fell 10%. It would take a sharp and unlikely contraction of the economy to repeat that scenario—a doubling of current mortgage rates and a halving of home sales—but if oil prices remain high, such a contraction is possible, according to Lawrence Yun, a forecast economist also with the National Association of Realtors.

After all, oil prices affect everything from how many workers a company hires to how much consumers pay at the pump. Given that the United States currently holds less than 2% of the world's oil reserves, and is faced with diminishing supply in places like Prudhoe Bay, it's likely that we'll have to ramp up imports. Analysts expect prices, which recently touched $60 a barrel, to remain high by historical standards over the next year or two.

Other factors are troubling, too. Americans are deeper in debt than ever before, many from risky interest-only and negative amortization loans they took out to take part in an all-night real estate party, which we'll discuss more in Chapter 2.

And the same herd mentality that has influenced manicurists to try to become real estate moguls could also swing the other way. One big bump-up in interest rates, coupled with a few local downturns, is all it would take to create a stampede for the exits. The effect could be devastating and widespread. In 2000, when the stock market fell, a third of the accumulated stock wealth was in the hands of 1% of investors. Today, the top 1% of home-equity holders control only 13% of the nation's housing wealth. When the housing market turns—and it always does, eventually—the manicurists and the moguls are going down together.

A TIME TO BUY, A TIME TO RENT

What should you do in these uncertain times, buy or rent? There's no one-size-fits-all answer, since it all depends on where you live, your income, your stage of life, and how often you plan to move. Generally speaking, people tend to rent when their income is the lowest, when they're young and old, and to own in-between. However, that's not always the case, especially today, when some young people are forgoing pricey cars and weddings to make down payments, some older people are opting to suck the equity out of their paid-off homes through reverse-equity mortgages, and some mid-career couples are renting in luxury condos in the city rather than buying a Mc-Mansion in the 'burbs.

A number of Web-based calculators can help you decide whether it's best to rent or own using data such as your salary, the cost of the home, the interest rate and term of the loan, and other factors. But bear in mind that many of these calculators are being offered by lenders who have a vested interest in your buying a home. One of the best calculators on housing affordability from a neutral source is on the Web site of Jack Guttentag, professor of finance emeritus at the Wharton School of the University of Pennsylvania. He also has other excellent calculators to help you determine the best ways to handle other mortgage scenarios, like comparing loans and fees, refinancing, consolidating debt, making extra payments to principal, terminating mortgage insurance, and figuring out the best loan terms. His Web site is www.mtgprofessor.com.

Let's look at the cases for owning and buying, so you can decide what best fits your current circumstances.

The Case for Owning

Uncle Sam wants you to own a house—badly. And he's willing to give you all sorts of incentives to convince you to do it. According to the Office of Management and Budget, homeowners currently get $76 billion annually through the mortgage interest deduction on their federal income tax returns and $14.8 billion through deductions for state and local property taxes. The agency says that mortgage interest deduction also saves owners an additional $29.7 billion on taxes on income that otherwise would be paid as rent.

What's more, if you sell your house after living in it for two out of the last five years, you get a tax-free gain: $250,000 for an individual, and $500,000 for a couple.

Because it's seen as a way to encourage responsibility and invigorate communities, homeownership is one of the few issues that truly enjoys bipartisan support. President Clinton introduced an initiative to increase the level of homeownership a decade ago; President Bush says he wants to create an "ownership society."

Under both administrations, the idea of renting has been given short shrift, even with populations that typically have rented, such as those with low incomes and shaky credit. "They're getting the message that they're losers if they don't buy," says Arlington, Virginia, housing economist John Tuccillo.

The Department of Housing and Urban Development currently gives home-buying help to low-income households through the American Dream Down Payment Fund, Self-Help Homeownership Opportunities Program, Section 8 Homeownership Vouchers, and the Section 32 Public Housing Homeownership option. HUD and the Neighborhood Reinvestment

Corporation also counsel renters who have the potential to become home buyers and encourage them to buy.

Uncle Sam's push toward home ownership has had its intended effect. Over the past decade, 10 million new households bought homes; now seven out of 10 American households live under their own roofs. That's certainly helped increase the average family's net worth at a time of stagnant wages and a lackluster stock market. Since the boom began in 1996, homeowners nationwide have amassed over $5.2 trillion in home equity.

More money means more choices, of course. Homeowners can take out their equity and use it for any purpose whatsoever, from paying for their kids' college education to subsidizing their Harley-Davidson habit.

Ownership also banishes many worries renters face about whether the landlord will raise the rent, withhold the security deposit, sell to Landlordzilla, or turn the building condo.

Plus, the politically sanctioned push toward homeownership, coupled with low interest rates and easy money from lenders, has caused builders to flock to for-sale housing and neglect the rental market. The supply of rental apartments is declining, as some are demolished due to age, and others are converted into condos. Construction of new rental housing fell to a 10-year low in 2004, as multifamily builders turned in droves to more lucrative condos.

Although rents are currently a bargain in some of the hottest housing markets (see "The Case for Renting," below), as supply tightens, that may soon change. It's happening already in some sizzling markets like south Florida, where condos are sprouting like kudzu, but long-term rentals are becoming as rare as jungle orchids.

In 2004, rents rose 4.2% after three years of stagnant growth of only 1% annually, according to Deerfield Beach, Florida, housing consultant Jack McCabe. Occupancy rates in Palm Beach County rose to 92% from 86.6% three years ago. Just a few years ago, a tenant could get concessions ranging from free rent to signing bonuses, but if you ask for them now "agents just laugh at you," Mr. McCabe says.

The Case for Renting

For those who already own a home, have built up equity, and live in the nation's hottest and most precarious housing markets, now may be a very good time to rent.

With price increases reaching the double digits in many metro markets, housing has become increasingly unaffordable. The National Association of Realtors' Housing Affordability Index was 132.6 in 2004, down from 138.4 the year before. By the second quarter of 2005, it had declined to 120.8.

In some markets, the flight to homeownership, spurred by low interest rates, has left units vacant, forcing landlords to make deals. In Atlanta, for instance, it's common to see giveaways of a month's rent. In Chicago, you can get two months' free rent and a $500 signing credit.

Overall, according to the National Association of Home Builders' Multifamily Market Outlook, the real rent index, adjusted for inflation, declined for the first four months of 2005 to 107.2, the lowest it's been since February 2003.

And in some of the most expensive for-sale markets in the country, rents have been falling even longer. Rents in San Francisco, for example, have fallen 19% since 2001, to $1,300. For that monthly rent, you currently can get a one-bedroom apartment on toney Nob Hill, with hardwood floors, a built-in china cabinet, and a courtyard with gazebo and built-in barbecue

Renting to Buy, Buying to Rent: Alyson Dutch's Story

A decade ago, Alyson Dutch, a public relations professional, moved to Malibu, California, to escape the pain of a divorce. She lived in a cramped place near the beach with her dog and cat until she spotted a charming compound of three homes under a canopy of ancient oaks. The three-bedroom main house was the residence of a former professional ballet dancer and his family; the apartment over the garage served as the owner's office; the one-bedroom guesthouse was for rent for the then-steep price of $2,000 a month. Ms. Dutch negotiated the rent down to $1,750, "upped my clients fees a bit, held my breath, and moved in."

What Ms. Dutch really wanted to do, however, was to buy the entire compound. And it turned out, the owner wanted to sell. But the $1 million price tag seemed hopelessly out of the reach for Ms. Dutch, at that cash-poor point in her life.

But bad timing can be overcome with a little ingenuity and seller help. The owner offered to give Ms. Dutch a note for 25% of the purchase price, at rates slightly higher than what a bank would charge, to use as a down payment. She financed the rest of the loan conventionally.

Ms. Dutch quickly found a renter for the main house. With the fresh cash flow, within two years she was able to refinance the property at a more favorable rate and pay off the owner's note.

Although her financial life is now in order, Ms. Dutch still lives in the guesthouse, uses the office over the garage, and rents out the main house. "The tenant's rent pays my entire mortgage and my taxes," she says, "so basically I live here for free."

grill. Meanwhile, buying a similar place costs about $530,000, or about $2,366 a month at a 5.34% interest rate—and that's assuming you put down $106,000, or 20% of the purchase price.

Despite its apple-pie image, homeownership has other drawbacks, too. Because renters typically pay less, they have more money to put in the stock market, businesses, and other investments, which helps not only them, but the economy as a whole. Renters also have flexibility, and can move without incurring heavy settlement costs, which typically run between 2% and 6% of the purchase price of a home.

By contrast, upscale owners in rising markets sometimes feel trapped in their homes by market forces. In Los Angeles, real estate broker Anthony Marguleas says that high property taxes and capital gains exclusions of only $250,000 for a single person and $500,000 for a couple means that sellers at the upper end of the market are "severely penalized." That discourages sellers from listing their homes, so "inventories stay low, while demand is very high."

Homeowners in stagnant markets can feel trapped, too, since they're paying higher prices to own but aren't building up any equity. Edward Tashjian bought a home in Hickory, North Carolina, seven years ago, but wishes he'd rented instead. "Hindsight is 20/20. It's barely appreciated," he says.

Buying has costs that renters don't need to think about, like homeowner's insurance, special assessments, and property taxes. Andrew Edson bought a second home in August 2004 in Boynton Beach, Florida, and was surprised to find that property taxes were 2% of the purchase price of his home. "It's a myth that low taxes prevail in Florida," he says. He closed just a few days before three successive hurricanes hit. As they barreled up the coast, he scrambled to find an insurer who would cover him. Although his home escaped major damage, the community he lived in did not, so he was hit with a special assessment to cover the damage not long after he moved in.

As Mr. Edson discovered, owners can be hit with many costs that come, like a hurricane, out of the blue. So though the real estate industry encourages renters to buy, if you're having trouble even making rental payments, stretching more could be a disastrous mistake.

Many families are already pushing their financial limits. According to the Department of Housing and Urban Development, housing is affordable if a moderate-income family spends no more than 30% of its income on shelter. But a recent study by the Joint Center for Housing Studies at Harvard University found that more than one in three households spend more than 30% on housing, while one in eight spend more than half.

Some lenders are trying to lure renters into homes by offering them risky interest-only or negative-amortization mortgages, which we'll look at more closely in Chapter 2.

But if you simply can't afford to buy without gambling your future, don't. "Many people are better off as lifetime renters," says economist John Tuccillo.

The Pros and Cons of Other Real Estate Investments

If you're worried about bubbles, there are other ways to invest in real estate without buying a home or condo. None of them should be attempted without expert financial help, and unless you have cash that you can afford to lose. Some possibilities:

REITs. Shorthand for Real Estate Investment Trusts, these are individual real estate companies that own and manage properties, and/or real-estate-backed loans. REITs invest in retail businesses, hotels, apartments, office buildings, industrial properties, manufactured housing, storage buildings, and other niche markets. According to the National Association of Real Estate Investment Trusts (NAREIT), REITs are now a $240 billion industry, up from only $12 billion a decade ago.

REITs issue shares and trade like stocks and bonds. By law, they must distribute 90% of taxable income in the form of dividends each year to shareholders.

In moderation, REITs are a good asset to have as part of a well-balanced portfolio, though analysts suggest keeping the proportion under 10%. Since REITs don't perform in tandem with stocks and bonds, they can help to offset losses when these markets are performing poorly.

Although they don't provide the sort of leverage you'd get if you owned a rental property directly, most REITs operate with about 50% debt, so right away you have a bigger equity stake in properties than you'd likely have if you'd purchased them outright.

REITs have been star performers for the last several years, riding up the real estate boom and yielding fat dividends, partly because they don't have to pay corporate taxes on them. In May 2005, the average REIT yielded 5.2%; the average 10-year Treasury bond returned only 3.9%.

In 2004, on a total return basis REITs rose 30.4% on average, beating most other stock indexes for the fifth year in a row. In the first five months of 2005, REITs were up 1.25%; the S&P 500 was down slightly.

But don't get too carried away acquiring REITs. Some analysts think they're victims of their own success, and have been bid up too high—at least for the moment. And REITs can be volatile—in 1998, after two years of strong returns, they suddenly tanked—then rallied again in 1999.

For more information, visit NAREIT's Web site at www. nareit.com.

REAL ESTATE MUTUAL FUNDS. Because real estate has been such a driver of the economy for so long, today you can choose from dozens of real estate mutual funds. These can be weighted toward commercial or residential rental properties, or a mix of the two. Some real estate mutual finds hold numerous REITs. If you're a small investor and want to diversify your REIT investments without incurring a lot of commission costs, real estate mutual funds are the way to go. Most mutual funds require an initial investment of $2,000, though some will accept as little as $250.

It makes sense to invest in funds that invest in the residential market when home prices are on the rise, and back off of them when the market has peaked. Commercial cycles often lag behind residential ones, however (see "Commercial Property," below), so you may want to switch funds to one more heavily invested in the commercial market once the residential market has started to decline. Before you invest, look at the fund's prospectus to check out its historical performance, management, price history, capital gains and dividends distribution schedule, domestic and international holdings, purchase minimums, expenses, and fees. A useful resource is www.inrealty. com.

REAL ESTATE HEDGE FUNDS. Real estate hedge funds have been around only since 2000, when GEM Realty Capital of Chicago launched the first one. You have to be well off, with a minimum net worth of $1.5 million, to invest in them. But if you have the cash to invest, returns can be substantial, topping 15%.

The goal of these hedge funds is to reduce some of the

volatility of REITs and other publicly traded property companies. They use both long and short positions, which helps mitigate swings in the marketplace. According to *Barron's*, real
estate hedge funds total about $500 million in assets.

But hedge funds are unregulated, so you shouldn't put any
money in them that you can't afford to lose. Before you invest,
talk to your financial advisor.

If you don't have a high net worth, you can still trade
"hedgelets" on www.hedgestreet.com. Here, people gamble on
the direction of mortgage rates, or home prices in various
major cities. The price of a hedgelet is always below $10, and
trades cost a flat fee of $5 for up to 100 hedgelets, and a nickel
per trade thereafter. HedgeStreet is regulated by the Commodities Futures Trading Commission, an independent agency of
the federal government.

REAL-ESTATE-RELATED STOCKS. The brightest spot in an otherwise weak stock market over the past five years has been
homebuilder stocks. During this period, shares of homebuild-
ing companies went up more than 50%, annualized, compared
with the average annual gains of REITs of 20% a year. Meanwhile, the Standard and Poor 500 was down 2%, annualized.

In fact, homebuilder stocks comprised seven out of the top
25 stocks over the last five years. And with inventories low,
builder stocks are still going strong. KB Homes in Los Angeles,
for instance, reported a 78% increase in profits for the second
quarter of this year. The home builder, which builds primarily
on the West Coast, as well as in Georgia, Florida, and France,
has had healthy increases in sales, price growth, and deliveries,
and the highest number of net new orders in the company's history. The company expects earnings for the year to reach $9 per
diluted share, up 14% over previous expectations.

Although builders are ramping up production, people are buying homes faster than builders can build them. According to the U.S. Census Bureau, unbuilt homes in developments where buyers can view plans or models are at their highest level since 1973, when the statistic was first tracked. In April 2005, the last month for which statistics are available at this writing, some 88,000 homes were for sale but not yet started, compared with 60,000 the year before, and 40,000 in 2000.

Although homebuilder stocks have benefited the most from the residential real estate run-up of the past five years, so to varying degrees have the stocks from publicly traded lenders, engineering firms, material suppliers, home-improvement re-tailers, insurance companies, property managers, real estate brokers, and others involved in the industry. As long as housing remains strong, so should the returns of companies that make their money in real estate. But if the market starts to turn, as we expect it will, so could these stocks.

LAND. Making money developing on raw land is a slow process, since getting the zoning and approvals can take years, espe-cially if neighbors object (and they usually do). Nevertheless, sowing brick-front Colonials where corn once grew is the retire-ment plan of many farmers today; the American Farmland Trust says that 1.2 million acres of agricultural land are lost to development each year.

One interesting option for individual investors is to buy fin-ished lots from developers. In many places, good building lots close to metro areas are scarce, and give a better return on in-vestment than developed properties. In Jackson Hole, Wyom-ing, for instance, single-family home prices rose 6% in 2004 over the year before, according to Brokerage of the Tetons, a real es-tate agency. But the average prices of home sites rose 38%.

Interior designer Peatt Raftis says the 1,600-square-foot home she bought in Port Ludlow, Washington, four years ago has appreciated 78% to $280,000. But a building lot in the same area that she could have purchased two years ago for $24,000 is now valued at $90,000, up 275%. Ms. Raftis wishes she had bought one then. "Lots seem to be where investors can make money now," she says.

COMMERCIAL PROPERTY. Commercial booms often follow residential ones, since businesses follow consumers. In Tucson, for instance, population has now reached the million mark, and businesses are moving in; overall occupancy in industrial parks rose a whopping 88% in 2004.

There are four major types of commercial real estate to consider: office, retail, industrial, and apartment buildings. Many investors shy away from them, because they don't have experience managing them, but good local commercial brokers and property managers can guide you.

Rent growth had been flat for the past few years, but according to a recent report by the National Association of Realtors, the near-term outlook is sunnier because supply is tightening. By 2006, office rents are expected to increase by 4.9%; retail by 3.2%, industrial by 2.53% and multifamily by 2.7%. (Some of the cities that are seeing the most growth, like Austin, Texas, are former "tech meltdown" markets that are now on the road to recovery, the report says.) That's not a fantastic return on your money, but one worth looking into should the residential real estate market head down.

You'll need to look at a number of factors before you buy, including zoning; pest, electrical, and environmental inspections; what sort of remodeling or improvements may be needed to meet tenants' needs and who will pay for it; parking; and restroom facilities. In Chapter 12 of Russ Whitney's *Millionaire Real Estate Mentor*, there's a good basic primer on commercial real estate investment; advice on fixing up apartments and other commercial buildings can be found in Robert Irwin's *Find It, Buy It, Fix It: The Insider's Guide to Fixer-Uppers*.

BOAT SLIPS. There are now more than 14 million boats on the nation's waterways, about a million more than there were in 2000. But because of tighter environmental regulations—building a marina can require permits from as many as 27 different governmental organizations—it's getting harder to find a place to park your dinghy, never mind your yacht.

Although the number of boats has grown, the supply of marinas has remained steady. And like everything else American, boats are getting bigger these days. The average length is 27 feet, too large to fit on a trailer.

As boaters scramble for slip space, investors are snapping them up. Prices in many places rival those of homes and so do the rates of appreciation—in Lee County, Florida, for instance, they've been appreciating at about 25% a year for the past decade. In Fort Myers, Florida, a 70-foot slip sold in 2004 for $450,000; the median home price for the area is $215,700.

Compared with owning a home, owning a boat slip is a lazy person's dream—you don't have to clean the gutters, replace the roof, or fix the furnace. In some of the swankier marinas that offer clubhouses, pools and tiki bars, however, you may have to pay monthly "condo" fees of $100 or more.

Some investors are paying six figures to own a slip that isn't even in the water. Drew Drake, a commercial real estate broker, recently bought a 45-foot-long boat slip for $155,000 in a "dockominium"—a dry storage area—at the Sanibel Harbor Yacht Club in Fort Myers. He doesn't even own a boat. "The location was great, and boat slips are so scarce, you can't beat this for a investment," he says.

SURVIVAL TIPS

• **Use seller financing.** This is often a win-win deal for both buyers and sellers, no matter how prices and interest rates are performing. If you're buying, ask if the seller will take back a note; you often can arrange more favorable terms than you could with a traditional loan. If you're selling, offer seller financing; you can often get a better rate of return than you could in other investments. If you don't want to take back the entire loan, consider offering a second mortgage to help buyers fill the gaps in financing. Just be sure to check credit scores and financial references carefully.

• **Move to a lower-cost area.** This doesn't necessarily mean giving up your expensive city digs for a place in the boonies.

As we saw in the last chapter, major cities follow different real estate cycles, so you can simply switch from Los Angeles to Washington, D.C., or Miami to take advantage of their relative spikes and peaks. (We'll talk more about how to figure out when a real estate market is on the upswing or downswing in the book's final chapter.)

But before you pull up stakes, take a look at everything that will factor into your cost of living, including salaries, groceries, transportation, entertainment, and other expenses. Some good cost-of-living and lifestyle-cost calculators can be found on www.homefair.com.

• **Skip the McMansion.** Real estate agents say that you should never build the grandest home in the neighborhood, because it simply won't appreciate at the same rate that it would if it were in a community of similar homes. Even if your home is in a community of older, modest homes that are being expanded and remodeled, it's better to wait until you see what the neighbors are doing, so you don't over-build.

• **Take a look at factory-built homes.** These are homes that are built in pieces in factories and then trucked to your lot, where they're put together by construction crews, then finished on site. Depending on the method used to build the home in the factory, the homes are referred to as "modular," "pre-cut" or "panelized."

Factory-built homes are more plumb and level than site-built homes. You'd think that this would make it easier for construction crews to assemble, but actually, carpenters make lots of adjustments for warped wood and other problems when they build traditional site-built homes that they can't make on factory-built ones. That's why it's important to make sure your construction crew is experienced in this sort of building, and certified by the factory.

When finished with siding, factory-built homes look the same as site-built ones, but they cost about 10% to 15% less, and can be finished in a third of the time. That's what convinced physician Andrew Harding to have a modular home constructed on a lot he owned in Bethesda, Maryland, a decade ago. He had some trepidation at first, especially when a flatbed truck with six modules and a crane showed up at 10 A.M. and all his neighbors came out with lawn chairs to watch the workers assemble the modules. "At 4 P.M., they were done with the basics, and handed me the keys to my house," he says. Today, his $300,000 investment has mushroomed in value to $900,000, about the same as similar site-built homes nearby. "I've never had any problems," he says. "I'd buy another modular home in a minute."

• **Don't rule out manufactured homes.** Once called "mobile" homes, manufactured houses aren't really mobile at all. They're built in one piece in a factory, then transported to a permanent site.

Though they'll never have the cachet of a site-built or a modular home, manufactured housing has come a long way from the ticky-tacky trailers of the past, thanks to the Manufactured Housing Improvement Act that Congress passed in 2000. Increasingly, manufactured housing isn't just a low-income choice, but is becoming attractive to middle-class workers and retirees. For instance, one 1,500-square-foot model built by Silvercrest Western Home Corporation, a California-based company, has vaulted ceilings, a kitchen island, formal dining room with bay window, covered patio, and two-car garage.

The best thing about a manufactured home is the price, which can be as low as half the cost of a site-built home or apartment. Because they're less costly than site-built homes, they're also usually the best deals for renters.

But there are downsides. It can cost much more to finance a manufactured home than it would a site-built one, especially if you are leasing the land. Resolving warranty issues can be difficult, too, since manufacturers sometimes blame installers for defects, and vice versa. For more tips, check www.consumersunion.org/mh.

SURVIVAL SUMMARY

- When trying to decide whether to buy or rent, pay attention to where you are in the real estate cycle.
- If you're only going to stay in an area for a couple of years or less, it's usually cheaper to rent than to buy.
- Look to buy when appreciation rates are a few points higher than the rate of inflation.
- Smooth out the peaks and valleys of local real estate cycles by diversifying into nondirect investments.
- When you want to buy or sell during a slow time in your local real estate cycle, use seller financing.
- When your market is peaking, sell and move to a lower-cost area.
- Look at alternatives to site-built homes, including factory-built and manufactured homes.

2

Buying under the Influence of Low Interest Rates

I knew the real estate market was getting out of control the first time I opened my Inbox and noticed that come-ons to take out a mortgage were outnumbering those for Viagra.

Yes, it is tempting to read about ads that promise me a loan for $550,000 for only $888 a month, or $229,861 at 3.05%, to mention just two that arrived in my e-mailbox this morning. And isn't it nice that the senders offered to "preapprove" me, or commit to give me a loan. Especially since I never met these alleged loan officers, never shared any details of my credit history or income, and never applied for a mortgage with them.

Spammers, of course, prey on our lusts. When the lust for

cheap money starts to outweigh simple lust, we should take it as a sign that we're all in trouble. And when it comes to sheer indebtedness, we are. According to Economy.com, accounting for inflation, household debt has more than doubled since 1990, to $10 trillion. Over the same period, household income has risen only 11%.

But the pain doesn't seem as severe is it might, because as rates have dropped over the last few years, we've continually tapped into our nest eggs. Serial refinancing has let us pay off everything from graduate school to that impromptu trip to the Cannes Film Festival.

We're also putting down less on our homes when we buy. According to the latest statistics available from the Federal Deposit Insurance Corporation, in 2003, 30% of all purchase mortgages written were for more than 80% of the home's price; in some cities, half of all borrowers took out this much.

Cheap money is the enabler of what has become an addiction to borrowing. From 2000 to 2004, average annual mortgage rates fell 28%. That set off a wave of borrowing that at this writing, is still going strong. Indeed, the Mortgage Bankers Association's Market Composite Index, a measure of mortgage loan application volume, recently reached 781, a record high.

Even though interest rates are at near-historic lows, home prices have risen so fast, they're still not affordable for many people. So creative financing deals from past decades are reappearing, including siren-song loans that offer zero interest, interest only, no down payment, no closing costs, optional payments, and many other combinations and variations. (Of course, there is no "free" loan as far as a lender is concerned—whatever you don't pay upfront, you'll have to pay later.)

Meanwhile, lenders are lowering their standards both in terms of the credit history of the borrower and the type of home they'll finance. "They've created mortgages that have allowed even sea slugs to buy housing," says Arlington, Virginia, housing economist John Tuccillo.

So-called "subprime" mortgages, made to people with less-than-sterling credit, increased tenfold in volume in the years between 1994 and 2003, according to the FDIC, and now account for more than 10% of all outstanding mortgage debt. While these loans have helped to increase the level of home-ownership to 69.1%, up from 67.1% five years ago, they also make the entire housing market inherently more unstable. Homeowners who already have shaky credit are more like to default, especially if they go through a stressful situation like divorce, illness, or job loss. Should the employment picture weaken, they'll be the first to go into foreclosure.

In stable times, lenders don't want to take back your home because it's a hassle and expense to resell. But in times of rapid appreciation, it becomes more worthwhile. Since they can resell quickly, their risk is lessened. So they're more willing than usual to lend us money to buy or remodel houses in iffy condition. In May, one lender told the *Oregonian* newspaper, "As things stand now, you could take a crack house and we'd lend you the money to fix it."

BORROWING IN YOUR UNDERWEAR

Not too long ago, lenders wouldn't give you a loan to buy a house unless you'd saved up 20% of the purchase price for a down payment. Most people got a fixed-rate mortgage, even if they knew they weren't going to stay in a home for the whole 30-year loan term. And they wouldn't refinance unless interest rates dropped at least two points.

These strategies seem quaint in today's adjustable or interest-only, no-down-payment, no-documentation lending environment. Now people track interest-rate fluctuations like they do stock tickers, refinancing if rates dip even a half point.

The change began in 1995, when Fannie Mae and Freddie Mac, government-sponsored entities that buy mortgage loans and repackage them for the secondary market, began to offer automated underwriting systems and other factors to evaluate borrower risk. One factor was FICO, a credit-scoring tool developed by the Fair Isaac Corporation, then called the Fair, Isaac Company. Lenders began using the systems and finally had a standardized way to evaluate customers they didn't actually know. Underwriting became streamlined. The era of long-distance lending was born.

Increased competition led to a wider variety of mortgage products and shaved lenders' profits. However, since many borrowers had no idea how their credit scores were compiled or what they were, many were still tentative about aggressively seeking lower rates and better terms.

But by 2001, consumers could access their own credit scores through the Web site Myfico.com. Finally, the veil had been lifted. Borrowers didn't have to dress up in suits and go through white-knuckled interviews with a number of bankers to know what sort of loan they could get. Moreover, they could apply for them at midnight in their underwear through such on-line bankers as E-Loan and Lending Tree.

In fact, Lending Tree was born when founder Doug Lebda, a certified public accountant, got the runaround from lenders when he and his wife tried to buy their first town house. "It was time-consuming, frustrating, and a hassle," he says. He operates the site much like a dating service for consumers, who fill out a form with their information, and lenders, who send their

"best deals" competing for their business. No one has to exchange so much as a handshake, which makes it much easier to
borrow, and borrow, and borrow again.

THE INTEREST IN INTEREST-ONLY LOANS

For many years, the standard loan has been the 15- or 30-year
amortizing loan.

Amortizing loans front load most of the mortgage's interest
payments in the early years of the loan's life, with a little bit of
principal paid off each month. Toward the end of the loan, the
balance switches, and more of the payments go toward reduc-
ing the principal owed. At the end of the loan period, you can
flick your Bic and burn the mortgage.

But recently, as home prices have rocketed out of sight, buyers have been looking for ways to lower monthly payments. A
growing number have been opting for "interest-only" loans instead of amortizing ones.

Interest-only isn't one type of loan—rather, it's an option
that can be added to any kind of loan, from 30-year fixed to one-
month adjustable. What it does, simply, is to put off the payment of any principal for a certain period, typically five, seven,
or 10 years.

Known to lenders as "IOs," these loans let you control a
property and deduct the interest payments. But because you
aren't paying toward your principal, you don't build any equity,
unless the value of your home rises. At the end of the interest-
only loan period, the balance becomes due. If you don't refinance, the loan becomes fully amortized.

Interest-only loans were the norm during the Roaring Twen-
ties. Back then, they weren't interest-only for a certain period,

but for the life of the loan. People just kept paying interest until they sold their homes, when, they hoped, appreciation would cover the cost of the mortgage and maybe provide a little profit, too. If they stayed in their homes a long time, they refinanced endlessly.

But when home prices fell during the Great Depression and wiped out equity, interest-only loans fell out of favor. Thereafter, most loans were written as fixed-rate amortizing loans.

This worked well for decades, because until recently, buyers tended to think of their homes and loans as long-term commitments. Owners got the advantage of a mortgage interest tax deduction when they were young and in their peak earning years. As they and their mortgages aged and no longer needed tax deductions, their equity increased.

Meanwhile, lenders still got most of their interest payments in the risky early years when buyers had the least equity and were most likely to default. For buyers, the advantage was that the loan was tantamount to a forced savings plan, ensuring that their stake in the home would grow over the years.

Nowadays, interest-only payments are back like bird flu. They're especially popular with first-time buyers who have been watching prices outpace their incomes. (According to Economy.com, housing costs increased 39% in the decade preceding 2003 for 18- to 25-year-olds, but their incomes only grew 29%.)

According to LoanPerformance, a San Francisco–based mortgage data firm, last year about a quarter of mortgages nationwide included an interest-only option, up from less than 2% four years ago, when the housing market first took wing. In some expensive markets, like Washington, D.C., and San Francisco, more than half of all loans are interest-only.

Even though they're usually offered at rates comparable with standard loans—or a little higher, typically around a quar-

When Money's Too Easy: A Lender's Tale

Ellen Bitton, chief executive officer of Park Avenue Mortgage Group with offices in New York and Palm Beach, Florida, has seen a lot of changes in her twenty years as a lender and mortgage broker. And she finds some of them "upsetting."

A decade ago, she says, when rates were in the 7% and 8% range, only wealthy people took out risky loans like interest-only mortgages. They used the money they saved on the mortgage to fund investments with higher rates of return, not to pay other bills. And if rates should go up? That might mean downsizing from a Maserati to a Lexus, but it wouldn't be a financial catastrophe.

Now, she says, "every Tom, Dick, and Harry is getting these loans, but they're not suited to everyone. Not everyone understands that rates can go up, or that equity can go down. Instead, they think, 'This is fun, cheap—I can afford more house.' "

Home equity lines of credit, or HELOCs, with variable-rate mortgages are even more dangerous to the average buyer, she says, if they don't realize how quickly they can rise.

Even more troubling, she says, is that so many lenders are doing everything they can to cash in on late-in-the-cycle profits; they're getting sloppy with their underwriting. Some are approving loans with debt-to-income ratios far above the usual 36%, going as high as 70% in some cases, and are making large numbers of loans without asking for any verification of income. Some even prefer not being bothered with paperwork, telling her, "A thin file is a good file."

Just about anyone can get a loan to buy anything these days,

(continued)

and that's not good. "My landscaper in the Hamptons told me he'd bought five houses," she says. "What's he doing buying all this?"

Saddest of all, she says, is that when everything inevitably comes to a head, the youngest and most vulnerable homeowners will be hurt the most. Older homeowners who remember the days of 14% and 15% mortgages are wary of risky loans, but younger ones aren't.

First-time borrowers are also too young to remember the bad old days of the early 1990s, when risky lending and a recession led to lenders' portfolios being stuffed with "real-estate-owned" properties, or REOs—otherwise known as foreclosures. When foreclosures increase, bankers become pessimistic and raise interest rates, leading to more foreclosures in a vicious cycle, she says. All it will take to start the cycle is for one bank to have a customer default on a large loan of $5 million or so. "When the first bank gets really burned, we're back in an REO world," she predicts.

ter of a percentage point—interest-only mortgages have lower payments in the early years. That's because you're deferring the payment of any principal. For instance, for a $250,000 30-year loan at 6%, the principal and interest of a standard, fully amortizing loan is $1,498. The monthly payment for an interest-only loan for the same amount is $1,250. The savings is $248.

But there's a price to be paid. If not refinanced or paid off, interest-only loans typically become fully amortized after a set period, and you have to pay both interest and principal, plus the principal you deferred. That's when your wallet really feels the impact. For example, if the interest-only loan in the above example becomes fully amortized after 10 years, the monthly payment will suddenly jump to $1,791 for the next 20 years, because you're paying both the regular and the deferred principal in a more compressed period. So to save $248 a month from the cost of a standard loan for the first 10 years, you have to pay $293 a month more for the next two decades.

This is fine if you're planning to sell your home before the interest-only period expires (and home prices haven't dropped in the meantime), or you're so sure that rates will go down that you'll be able to refinance, or you expect a big fat raise, or you have a surefire investment that brings better after-tax returns than the cost of the loan, or you're really, really lucky at bingo.

Or if you're incredibly disciplined like Adam Brauer, president of Debtsettlementusa.com, who took out a $385,000 interest-only loan in April when he bought a two-bedroom condo in Cliffside Park, New Jersey. However, he's treating it like an amortizing loan by sending the extra $1,000 he "saves" each month to the lender as a payment toward the principal. He doesn't have to do this every month, so he has more flexibility than he'd have with a standard loan. "Hey, I'm human; I like to splurge sometimes," he says. But when the loan finally reaches the amortization period, he'll have built up some equity and the payment won't seem shocking.

PULLING MONEY FROM THE WALLS

Perhaps it was too much to expect homeowners to keep their hands off their home's equity in an era of double-digit price gains.

Certainly, lenders have been eagerly encouraging them to pull money out of their rapidly appreciating walls. On its Web site, Fremont Bank entices its equity-rich San Francisco Bay area customers to "use your equity to get more from life," suggesting that they use the money for such things as remodeling and education.

Lenders are stretching the loan-to-value ratio, too. In the past, loan-to-value ratios were usually limited to 80%, including both your first mortgage and your home-equity loan. So, if your home was worth $200,000, and you had a $100,000 first mortgage, you could borrow an additional $60,000. Now some lenders, like East West Mortgage in McLean, Virginia, are letting customers borrow up to 125% of their home's equity in what it calls its "debt-crusher loan" with rates advertised as "much better than those credit cards."

But federal banking regulators have issued guidelines to lenders warning them to be more careful about providing easy money, particularly to people with shaky credit. The warning was specifically directed at home-equity loans, though similar guidelines are expected soon for purchase mortgages.

Equity loans currently have low rates of default, but regulators are worried that this might not always be the case. Right now, they're often being made as interest-only loans, at high loan-to-value or debt-to-value ratios. Lenders don't require as high credit scores as they do for primary mortgages. They also rely heavily on third parties like mortgage brokers to check out borrowers' creditworthiness, and don't require much documentation of income. Regulators fear that loans are being given to people who'll get into financial trouble should interest rates spike.

Here are some ways borrowers have been pulling equity out of their homes:

CASH-OUT REFINANCING. Cash-out refinancing is simply a new loan. It adds whatever amount of home equity you want to borrow, plus settlement costs, to the outstanding principal balance of your previous mortgage. Your old mortgage is paid off.

Before cashing out your old mortgage, you need to find out if this option is cheaper than simply getting a home-equity loan, also known as a second mortgage. If the cash-out refi's interest rate is lower than the existing rate on your loan, it's likely to be cheaper than a home-equity loan.

Although most cash-out refis are routine affairs, sometimes a dishonest lender will dangle a large amount of cash in front of an unsophisticated, equity-rich owner without the means to pay it back. The lender tacks excess "junk" fees onto the loan, which bumps up the monthly payment. When the owner defaults, the lender takes back the house, sells it, and hoovers up the equity.

HOME-EQUITY LOAN (SECOND MORTGAGE). A home-equity loan is a second mortgage secured by your home. It gives you the money in a lump sum.

Because it's paid off after a first mortgage in the case of default, it's riskier to lenders and typically carries a higher interest rate—but not always. Unlike first mortgages, which are typically bundled together and sold as mortgage-backed securities to Wall Street investors, home-equity loans are usually kept in the lender's own portfolio.

Many homeowners like this type of loan because you can choose either a fixed or an adjustable rate. Settlement costs are similar to a first mortgage, though some lenders will reduce or eliminate them, especially if you have your primary loan with them.

Unlike primary mortgages, the interest rates on these loans are based on short-term bond yields, such as those of two- or five-year Treasuries, and are sensitive to the federal funds rate controlled by the Federal Reserve (which has been raising it lately in small increments).

HOME-EQUITY LINE OF CREDIT (HELOC). This is a line of revolving credit on your home with a variable rate. You can pay off the costs and then borrow again against the line without taking out another loan. Borrowing charges are low, and some lenders waive them altogether.

Terms for HELOCs range from five to 30 years. Many lenders base the rate on the *Wall Street Journal* prime rate, which moves in tandem with the federal funds rate.

Lenders set up HELOCs with two time periods. The first, a draw period, usually lasts between five and 10 years. During this time, you can borrow against it, and your monthly payments cover only interest, although you can add more to pay off part of the principal. After this comes a repayment period, often a decade or more, when you can't borrow against the line and must pay down the balance of the loan. Payments change depending on the interest rate, how much you owe, and whether you're in a draw or repayment period. Some lenders insist that you pay off the entire balance immediately after the draw period.

Be careful when you're shopping for a HELOC to ask what the margin is between the prime rate and what you'll be paying. Truth-in-Lending laws do not require lenders to disclose this. Depending on your credit score and other factors, it may be less attractive than what the lender is advertising. Also ask if there are any rules governing minimum balances or initial draws, and any fees to service or cancel the account.

Unlike adjustable rate mortgages, which change only after set periods like one, three, or five years, HELOCs adjust the first day of the month after a change in the prime rate.

FINANCING GETS CREATIVE—AGAIN

Back in the 1980s, when mortgage interest rates climbed as high as credit card rates are now, creative financing schemes abounded. Now they're back for a different reason, so that people can afford to pay home prices that have rocketed out of their reach. Doug Duncan, chief economist of the Mortgage Bankers Association, says there are about 150 different types of loan products currently on the market, and no way to keep track of them all. "Some are very esoteric and not widely used," he says.

Although these loans help buyers afford homes they otherwise wouldn't qualify for, most carry much more risk than the standard fixed-rate 15- or 30-year loan. Their return worries some experts. "If you're not knowledgeable and sophisticated about these mortgage products, you'll get burned," says Frank Nothaft, chief economist of Freddie Mac.

Below is a list of the creative financing vehicles being pushed by many lenders that require a good deal of caution on the part of borrowers. Some are fairly new; others are making a reappearance. If you're considering them, be sure to calculate true costs—a number of good mortgage calculators can be found on Web sites, like www.mortgage-x.com, www.mortgage101.com, www.fmcalcs.com, and www.freddiemac.com. For an overview of calculator Web sites with links, check out www.martindale center.com. For more information, check out these excellent books: *The Common-Sense Mortgage* by Peter G. Miller, *The Mortgage Encyclopedia* by Jack Guttentag, and *100 Questions Every First-Time Home Buyer Should Ask* by Ilyce Glink.

NEGATIVE-AMORTIZATION LOANS. These come in a number of flavors and are behind many of the low-rate teaser ads that are flooding our Inboxes of late.

What they have in common is a monthly payment that's insufficient to pay off the loan by the end of its term. The shortfall is added to the loan balance, so what you don't pay in the beginning, you pay later. If home prices don't rise enough to cover the growing loan amount, and you have to sell because of a job transfer or some other reason, you can wind up owing more than the house is worth. Lenders call that being "upside down" or having "negative equity."

Some loans with negative amortization end with a balloon payment, when the whole enchilada becomes due and you have to either pay up or refinance. Others begin to amortize at some point so the principal can be repaid.

One plan, known as the graduated-payment mortgage or GPM, is coming back after being abandoned by lenders for almost two decades. Invented to help first-time buyers afford a home, it starts at a low rate and increases each year by a certain percentage—say, 6% a year for five years. Then the rate is set for the rest of the loan period, and the loan begins to amortize. This gives buyers who expect their income to rise, or who don't plan to live in their home very long, a chance to buy the most expensive house possible for the lowest possible monthly payments.

Another plan is called an "option" adjustable-rate mortgage. This type of loan allows several different payment options, including paying less than the interest payment alone, for a short period. For obvious reasons, this is the loan of choice for home flippers who are planning to sell in less than a year. But it's also popular with buyers who focus on monthly payments rather than long-term costs and risks.

ARMs with negative amortization typically will have either a very low teaser rate, a cap that could prevent monthly payments from covering increases in interest rates, or payment adjustments that don't keep pace with rate adjustments—or all three.

Since lenders don't want you to walk away from the house and your obligations, ARMs typically limit the amount of negative amortization to no more than 125% of the original loan. When this limit is reached, the low payment party is over, and you have to start paying off the difference.

Although negative-amortization loans can be useful if you know you're only going to own your home a short time, for the most part it's best to avoid them. If you really are in a cash-flow crunch, especially in an unstable real estate market, it may be better just to sell your home and rent.

And remember: Many lenders won't allow second mortgages on properties with negative-amortization loans, so even if your equity does rise over time, you won't be able to spend it.

ZERO-INTEREST LOANS. Generally available only through home builders or sellers offering private financing, these short-term loans—usually for no more than seven years—seem strange on the surface. Where's the profit if there's no interest?

The answer is, from a bigger price tag on the home.

The deal works this way: The seller asks for a big down payment and an above-market price for the home. He sells the note to an investor at a discount, but not so big a markdown that he walks away with less cash than he would have collected in a conventional mortgage deal. The investor collects on the note from the buyer.

Who wants these loans? Mostly the well-off, who can handle high monthly payments and a big down payment. Big spenders like them, too, since they can get away with higher debt-to-income ratios than usual (the seller gets his money quickly and doesn't worry about default). And because no interest is paid, the overall costs are only a fraction of what a conventional mortgage costs.

But what about that wonderful gift from Uncle Sam, the

mortgage interest deduction? Actually, the Internal Revenue Service expects lenders to charge interest on a loan, and so may calculate "imputed interest" on such deals. This interest can be deducted, if the borrower isn't subject to the Alternative Minimum Tax. The rules on imputed interest are complex and changing, so it's advisable to check with a tax specialist or certified public accountant. The IRS updates information on imputed interest on its Web site, www.irs.gov.

SHARED-APPRECIATION MORTGAGE (SAM). This loan matches homeowners with investors, who agree to buy down the interest rate, fund a down payment, or provide other kinds of financial help. In return, the investor shares in any profit once the home is sold. These tend to be private deals, and are hard to find. In the past, some investors entered into them because they could participate in a rising real estate market without the hassles of being a landlord. But when the market tanked, they lost out. Today, investors who don't want to be awakened in the middle of the night whenever their tenant's toilet overflows are more likely to buy into a professionally managed real estate investment trust.

WRAPAROUND FINANCING. Usually a form of seller financing, this is used when a buyer wants to keep the seller's original low-interest, assumable loan. The buyer gets a second loan that makes up the difference that lasts the remaining term of the loan. Additionally, the buyer offers to pay the seller (or in some cases, a wraparound lender) a rate of return that's higher than the payment rate of the original loan. The seller or wraparound lender makes the original loan payment each month.

This deal can be a win-win situation, with both seller and buyer benefiting, when interest rates are high or rising. However, there can be confusion when it comes to taxes, property assessments, and the order of repayment in case of default. Moreover, if the seller doesn't make the original loan payment each month, the property could go into default. If the buyer

A "SAM" Gone Sour: The Fitzpatricks' Story

Creative marketing schemes abound when either mortgage interest rates or home prices get too high. Often, they're the only way buyers can afford homes when the market gets wacky. But when the market sours, often so do these schemes.

At least, that's what Patrick and Eileen Fitzpatrick discovered. In the late 1980s, prices in the Virginia suburbs of Washington, D.C., were climbing. After a long search, the Fitzpatricks finally found a brick contemporary that was big enough for their blended family with six children. But though they could just make the monthly payments on a loan at 10%, the prevailing interest rate, they just couldn't afford the down payment. Nor could they afford to spruce up the house, which was a bit run-down.

So they took their real estate agent's advice and were matched with an investor in a shared-appreciation mortgage, popularly known as a SAM. In this case, the Fitzpatricks paid the mortgage and provided sweat equity for home improvements. The investor put up the 20% down payment and agreed to pay for the cost of materials for improvements if they ran over $300. In return, he was promised his down payment back, plus half of the profits when the house sold.

Over the next five years, the Fitzpatricks replaced everything from the wallpaper to the carpets. But by then, prices had begun

(continued)

to fall. Panicked, the Fitzpatricks sold the house for $160,000, the same price they'd paid for it. With no profit, they had to repay the investor out-of-pocket for his down payment, plus settlement costs. Neither the investor nor the Fitzpatricks won this financial game. "My husband was afraid if we waited, we'd lose even more," Mrs. Fitzpatrick recalls.

doesn't pay, the seller has to go through the hassle of foreclosure.

Like wraparound dresses, wraparound mortgages aren't as popular as they were in the 1980s. That's because these days, only loans guaranteed by the Federal Housing Administration or the Veterans Administration can be easily assumed (though you do have to meet these agencies' lending standards, and some fees are involved). Most lenders grit their teeth at the idea of wraparounds, because they'd prefer to retire low-interest loans and replace them with more lucrative ones.

PIGGYBACK LOANS. These relatively new and very useful loans graft home-equity loans onto primary loans so you can get away with the lowest possible down payment and still avoid private mortgage insurance, also known as PMI. PMI is required whenever you put down less than 20% when you buy a home, and it can amount to as much as $500 a year on a $100,000 mortgage. (Though you have to pay PMI, it doesn't protect you from anything—rather, it indemnifies the lender if you default.) Of course, you'll pay a little higher interest rate on the home-equity loan. But hey, it's tax deductible, unlike PMI.

LEASE-OPTION. This is one of the best ways to buy or sell a home, especially in uncertain times, according to California attorney and housing writer Bob Bruss. The deal can take many forms. In one common scenario, the buyer agrees to rent a home at an above-market rate for a set period. The owner puts the difference between the payment and the rent into an interest-bearing escrow account. At the end of the lease period, should the owner decide to sell, the tenant gets first dibs. The money from the escrow account goes toward the down payment. A third-party lender provides the rest of the financing, or the seller takes back a note.

The terms of a lease-option can be whatever the buyer and seller negotiate. For instance, when I bought my first house with a three-year lease-option, the seller and I agreed on a price for the house at the beginning of the lease period. Because the house appreciated over three years, I wound up buying at a discount. I saved thousands. But he saved, too, because he didn't have to pay a real estate agent to find him a buyer for his home.

GOVERNMENT-SUBSIDIZED LOANS

Uncle Sam wants you to own a home. That's why the interest on your mortgage is tax deductible. That's also why there are agencies on the local, state, and federal levels devoted to helping financially struggling buyers find homes.

Nationally, there are also special mortgage products developed by the Department of Housing and Urban Development (HUD), as well as government-sponsored enterprises Fannie Mae and Freddie Mac to help low- and moderate-income buyers find homes. Some are niche products aimed at schoolteachers, police officers, Native Americans, rural residents, the disabled, seniors who want to take out home equity, folks who buy energy-efficient homes, and even people who want to live

near public transit. You can find out more about these programs by visiting the Web sites www.hud.gov, www.fannie
mae.com, and www.freddiemac.com.

GOING LONG: THE 40-YEAR LOAN

To get the lowest possible monthly payment, you can extend the
term of servitude to your mortgage to 40 years. Both fixed-rate
loans and ARMs can be packaged this way, including negative-
amortization ARMs.

While 40-year loans have been around for more than two
decades, only a few lenders have wanted to make them, because
they couldn't be bundled and sold to Wall Street through the
secondary mortgage market. But that changed in the summer
of 2005 when Fannie Mae, which buys about one out of every
four loans from lenders, said it would start buying them (it already had been buying them on a small scale from some credit
unions). Its cousin in the mortgage-bundling trade, Freddie
Mac, is considering buying them, too.

The mortgages have rates comparable to those of interest-
only loans, and do have the advantage of accruing principal
(which means that monthly payments will be higher than you'd
pay for an interest-only note). But the dark side is, you'll be giving your lender a gigantic gift of interest before the loan is paid
off, assuming you keep it until the bitter end. You'll also pay a
slightly higher interest rate than you would on a 30-year loan,
typically a quarter point or more. And you'll build equity more
slowly.

You don't save that much each month if you get a 40-year
loan instead of a conventional loan. For instance, the difference
in monthly payments between a 30-year mortgage for $100,000
at 6% and a 40-year version of the same loan at 6.25% is only

$32. But you'll owe $56,676 more in interest over the life of the loan. If you keep the loan only seven years, the average amount of time a homeowner lives in a home, the 40-year loan will cost $1,177 more.

BURNISHING YOUR CREDIT RATING

Calling Jimmy Stewart: Mortgage lending is no longer the warm and personal experience it was in the movie *It's a Wonderful Life*. Nowadays, all of your financial habits are reduced to a number: your FICO score. That magic number directly impacts what sort of deal you'll get on your mortgage, and even what sort of lender will consider you as a client. FICO scores run from 300 to 850, with higher rates indicating a better credit risk. Score anything under 700, and your rates go up; under 600, and you may have trouble getting a loan from a legitimate lender.

Credit scores are weighted according to the following formula: 35% on your past payment history; 30% on how much you owe others; 15% on the length of your credit history; 10% on whether you've applied for or recently opened new credit cards; and 10% on other assorted factors, like the mix of credit you carry (for example, auto loans, personal lines of credit, credit cards, and mortgages). By law, they can't take into account race, color, national origin, religion, gender, or marital status.

Three different agencies keep track of your borrowing habits: Equifax, Experian, and TransUnion. Each will have a different score for you. Lenders might check just one of these agencies or all three, so it pays to keep track of what they say about you. You can get the scores by contacting each of the three agencies, or contacting www.annualcreditreport.com—a recently enacted federal law requires the agencies to give you one free report each year. Or you can pay Myfico.com $14.95 for one FICO score, or $44.85 for all three. Although you also can get your FICO score for free from a lender when you apply for a loan, it's better to check it yourself beforehand; that way you'll have time to correct errors. If you find a mistake, contact both the credit agency and the creditor who reported the error.

You can do other things, too, to polish up your credit score before taking out a mortgage:

- **Pay your bills on time.** Every delinquency is going to hurt your score.

- **Pay down as much debt as you can.** That may mean that you'll have to take out a larger mortgage, but the interest rate on a home loan will be lower than a credit card—and it's tax-deductible.

- **Don't apply for new credit cards.** You'll need at least some debt history to have a FICO score, but the creditors want to make sure you're not wallowing in debt, or switching balances from one card to another.

- **Don't take out any big loans.** Although some shady mortgage lenders will let customers take on too much debt so they can repossess the house, legitimate lenders don't want to see you stretched too thin. As a rule of thumb, no more than 36% of gross monthly income should be going toward debt.

SURVIVAL TIPS

- **Question "teaser" rates.** Some lenders play a "bait-and-switch" game with interest rates, advertising rates that are good only for a short time or for borrowers with flawless credit. Make sure the lending officer sends you the terms of the deal he or she plans to give you in writing.

• **Watch out for the closing cost hustle.** If you've got a first mortgage with a lender, you'll probably get a break on closing costs when you refinance, because the lender doesn't have to repeat many of the underwriting procedures. But if you own your house free and clear, the lender will have to go through all the steps required for a first mortgage, and may try to make you pay.

• **Lock your loan rate.** Unless you're an interest rate junkie who checks fluctuations daily, it doesn't make sense to try to "float" your loan rate. Also, ask if the lender charges a fee to lock the loan; not all do.

• **If you use a mortgage broker, make sure the lender sends you the lock rate in writing.** When rates decline, some unscrupulous brokers quote you a higher rate than you can actually get yourself directly from the lender, then pocket the difference; but when they rise, they renege on the deal.

• **Get an extended lock period.** Mortgage rates have been turbulent, and refinance activity is high. Loan officers, appraisers, and title insurers are swamped with business. So it's possible that your lock period can run out before the loan is closed. Ask your lender to give you a timeline indicating when each step of your loan will be completed. Make sure you get a loan lock period of at least 60 to 90 days.

• **Resist paying off unsecured debt with secured debt.** Although the rates are lower and the interest tax deductible, think twice before replacing unsecured debt, like credit cards, with secured debt, like a mortgage. If you default on unsecured debt, the worst that could happen to you would be the revocation of your credit card. But if you don't pay a mortgage, you could lose your home.

• **Pay off more of the principal each month.** Sure, it may require brown-bagging it or ironing your own clothes rather than taking them to the dry cleaners, but you can cut your mortgage term considerably by making extra principal payments each month. For instance, for less than $10 a day, you can reduce the term of a $250,000 fixed-rate 30-year loan at 6% to 20 years. By adding an extra $298.08 a month to the standard principal and interest payment of $1,498.88, you'll have your mortgage-burning party a decade earlier. And you'll save $108,805.81 over the life of the loan.

• **Pay biweekly.** Paying your loan every other week, instead of once a month, adds the equivalent of one extra monthly payment per year. Doing this will reduce the length of your loan term and cut down on the amount of total interest you will pay over the life of the loan. (However, some lenders will charge you extra set-up or servicing fees to handle biweekly payments.)

• **Don't extend your payment term length when you refinance.** If you're planning to live in your house awhile, but want to refinance when rates are low, ask the lender to reamortize your current loan. You'll save thousands in interest.

• **Calculate the break-even point.** Before you jump on that tempting low-interest loan, figure out how long it will take you to recoup your out-of-pocket costs. Divide those costs (including any points and settlement costs) by the amount of money you'll save monthly with the new loan. That will tell you how many months it's going to take for you to break even. If you're going to sell before then, it's not worth it.

• **Pay attention to fees.** Lenders sometimes pump up their profits at the closing table by adding fees, called "junk" or "garbage" fees in the trade. For instance, you may be charged hundreds of dollars for having your document faxed or printed out from a computer, or sent by bike messenger across town. The whole question of fees has become so controversial that at least one major lender, Bank of America, recently introduced a program called Mortgage Rewards, which waives fees for the loan origination, application, appraisal, flood determination, tax service, and others. (It doesn't pay for title insurance, however.) The bank estimates borrowers can save about 1% on a $200,000 loan. Other major lenders like Countrywide will guarantee its fees are the same you receive in your Good Faith Estimate.

• **Consider the worst-case scenario.** If you're thinking about taking anything other than a fixed-rate loan, you're assuming risk. Calculate what you'd owe monthly and overall in the worst-case scenario.

• **Get rid of private mortgage insurance as soon as possible.** If you pay less than a 20% down payment on a loan, you'll usually have to pay private mortgage insurance (PMI). Federal law requires lenders to cancel this insurance when your equity reaches 22%, but you can get it canceled as soon as it reaches 20% if you pay for an appraisal. Lenders won't cancel PMI on a loan you've held for less than 24 months. Mortgage insurance on loans guaranteed by the Federal Housing Administration can never be canceled.

SURVIVAL SUMMARY

- Beware of lenders who offer low teaser rates.
- Understand that money that's below-market now will cost you more later.
- Don't let the prospect of low monthly payments blind you to the true overall cost of a teaser-rate loan.
- When taking an adjustable- or variable-rate mortgage, be sure you understand all of its terms. Calculate a worst-case scenario.
- In general, risky loans that have low monthly payments only make sense if you plan to stay in your home a short time, or expect you'll be able to refinance at lower rates.
- Avoid loans with negative amortization, especially if it looks like interest rates will rise and house prices have peaked.
- To boost your credit rating and get the best interest rates from lenders, pay down debt and don't open any new credit cards.
- When comparing mortgages, pay attention to the lender's settlement costs and fees.

3

Your Secret Agent: You

Do you really need a real estate agent?

A decade ago, few people would have even asked the question. About the only way to see what was available for sale was to go to a local real estate agent, who prescreened and printed out listings from the local multiple listing service.

All that has changed. You no longer have to go through a full-service agent to view homes for sale anywhere in the country—the information is as easy to find on the Internet as Paris Hilton photos. Nearly all of the nation's multiple-listing-service listings, some 2 million in all, are shown on www.realtor.com, so buyers can do their own prescreening. If you're a seller, you don't need to go to a full-service broker to be listed there—you can go to a flat-free broker, or a discount broker who will do the job for a commission as low as 2%.

And if you don't want to have anything at all to do with real estate brokers, you can go to the parallel universe of for-sale-by-owner (FSBO) Web sites that have sprung up over the last few years, with names like www.owners.com, www.forsalebyowner.com, and www.fsbo.com.

In other words, buying real estate, like buying gasoline, clothing, insurance and nearly everything else, increasingly has become self-service.

So why are most of us still paying 5% or 6% commissions, just like we did ten years ago?

It's an especially relevant question in this current climate of price run-ups and bidding wars, when agents don't have to do more than list the house, write down the offers, and collect the commission. Many in the hottest markets don't even have to spring for advertising costs, since they sell within hours of listing.

And as home prices have soared, commissions have, too. Existing-home sales posted a 12th consecutive record in 2004, with $5.6 billion worth of transactions. In a neighborhood with 15% annual appreciation, the country's median at this writing, someone who sold a house last year for $600,000 would have paid a 6% commission of $36,000 to the listing agent, who would then split it with the listing broker and selling agent. This year, that same house would sell for $690,000, and a 6% commission would be $41,400.

Not many people got a 15% raise last year. That's one reason why so many people have been racing to get their real estate licenses. Nationwide, the number of real estate agents has grown to more than a million, a 10% increase over 2004, according to the National Association of Realtors.

As inexperienced agents flood the field, and experienced ones become order-takers, many sellers are asking the question: What are agents doing now—what could they *possibly* do—to justify such an increase?

It isn't because agents have more work to do than before. Walt Molony, spokesman for the Realtors trade group, says agents don't spend as much time as they used to finding or showing homes to buyers, because buyers increasingly are identifying the homes they want to see on the Web. Nor do they spend as much time as they used to filling out forms and paperwork, since that, too, has become more automated and efficient.

It's also questionable whether agents bring buyers better prices. The trade group says agents bring prices that are 15.4% higher than sellers who don't use one. But in their book *Freakonomics,* University of Chicago economist Steven D. Levitt and coauthor Stephen J. Dubner note that when agents put their own homes on the market, they leave them on for 10 more days and sell them for 3% more than the homes of their clients. The book also purports that agents use vague words like "fantastic" and "charming" to describe their clients' houses, rather than stronger, more specific adjectives, because their primary goal is to persuade homeowners to sell for less than they'd like, and alert buyers that the house can be had for less than the listing price.

Mr. Molony disputes the notion that agents are just out for a quick commission. "Their business relies on their reputation for getting the highest price for their clients," he says. He adds that agents add value in handling tricky people problems and details that may trip up inexperienced sellers. "A FSBO doesn't have someone to handle negotiations or find a middle ground when emotions run high," he says. "He doesn't have someone who will tell him what disclosures he needs for his house in his state, or who will keep his house secure by prescreening buyers."

Although the trade association doesn't keep track of commission levels, Mr. Molony says that anecdotally, commission percentages seem to be dropping. In the Midwest, where price growth has been positive but not overwhelming, commissions have been running around 6%; in the hot Northeast, they're running around 4%. "It's driven by the marketplace," he says.

Part of what's pushing down costs is the popularity of flat-fee brokers and discount brokers. These give general bare-bones help, rebates, or menu-based options at reduced cost. Most important, many do what owners can't do for themselves, which is get the house listed on local multiple listing services. But after that, sellers get a break depending on what aspect of their home's marketing and sale they want to assume on their own, such as advertising, holding open houses, negotiating, or handling the paperwork.

At least one national broker, Ziprealty, which started in 1999, is relying on a Web-based business model that treats agents as employees rather than independent contractors, to help hold down costs. Marketing is somewhat bare-bones, but covers the basics: home advertisements in local newspapers and on real estate Web sites with virtual tours, one open house, one for-sale sign on the lawn, flyers, an e-mail blast to buyers, and coordination of showings. Its rates, however, are typically 1% less than the going rate in an area—for the $690,000 house we talked about earlier, Ziprealty's commission would be $34,500, 17% less than what a broker charging a 6% commission would receive. Other discount or flat-fee brokers include Help-U-Sell and Assist-2-Sell.

But full-service brokers are doing all they can to keep tight control over the money machine. The National Association of Realtors once proposed a rule that would allow real estate agents to prevent their listings from being displayed on the Web sites of any brokers they chose (meaning discount brokers). But pressure from federal regulators and discount broker members convinced them to withdraw it.

Meanwhile, government antitrust legislators have been looking into industry-backed initiatives in several states that would limit lower-cost options for consumers. Within the last year, a number of those initiatives have passed. For instance, Oklahoma recently enacted a minimum-service law that will bite into menu-based brokerages by requiring, among other things, that agents present all offers and counteroffers.

SHOW AND TELL

Whether you use an agent or sell the house yourself, you'll need to market it. Naturally, that means using all the traditional tools like yard signs, flyers, and classified ads in local newspapers. But two important marketing rules aren't so well known:

- **Skip the open house.** You'll have to have the place sparkling for showings, of course, but there's really no need for a weekend open house. Open houses are really a way for agents to meet new customers. Only 2% of buyers find the house they eventually purchase that way, according to the National Association of Realtors. Plus, an open house attracts thieves, who often travel in pairs, with one distracting the owner or agent while the other pockets valuables. Some thieves also use the occasion to case your premises, so they can burglarize it later.

  However, if you use a brokerage to sell your house, insist that they put your house on the weekly "caravan" list. That's when agents drive to different new listings to check them out in person (the listing agents usually provide platters of cold cuts or other goodies to make a good impression, so the event has the feel of a progressive dinner party). Because they've previewed these homes, the agents will show them first; they also trade notes on likely buyers at these events.

• **Go high-tech.** About three-quarters of all home buyers shop for homes on the Web these days, according to the National Association of Realtors. If you list with a Realtor, your home probably will appear on the country's biggest listing site, www.realtor.com, as well as the local brokerage's Web site, and possibly the agent's individual Web site, if he has one. Pretend you're a buyer and do a browser search to see if the Web site of the brokerage you're considering shows up high in the responses—no one is going to scroll through several pages. Look for agents who will spring for the cost of a virtual tour—some shoppers will only look at homes that have one.

But don't stop there—if you're technically gifted or know someone else who is, put up your own Web site, with as many pictures as possible.

Or if you really always wanted to direct, videotape a tour of a home with a soft background sound track or narrative description of your home, and burn some CDs for out-of-town home shoppers.

STAGING, OR "ROMANCING THE HOME"

No matter how buyers get to your home, what really matters is what they see when they get there. So here's where your job really gets hard, especially if you're in a cooling market.

Thanks to the explosion of shelter magazines and television

home decorator shows over the last five years, we've all been exposed to fabulous images of perfectly coordinated homes.

It's really difficult to compete with these fantasies of artfully fluffed duvets and $500 raw silk throw pillows, but you must try. One good way to start is to look at the competition that sets the standards for your neighborhood—the nearest new home community.

When I first started writing about home building in 1984 as feature editor of *BUILDER* magazine, a trade publication, model home decoration wasn't very sophisticated. Some builders left their models vacant. Others bought up room settings at the local JCPenney and had them shipped straight to their models. Their wives were enlisted to hang pictures and make the furniture fit.

Today, model-home merchandising is a multimillion-dollar business dominated by a few talented interior designers you've never heard of, because they work only for home builders. Using the builder's focus group and consumer research, these designers create fictional families for each model, work out what the hobbies and interests of each member of the family might be, and order furnishings and accessories to match, down to the fake soccer trophies and matching soccerball-patterned soap dishes and shower curtains in the kids' wing. The idea isn't just to fill the model with furniture but to give it a personality—to make it seem like the buyer's fantasy home.

Well, you may be saying now, my home is just overflowing with personality and the detritus of hobbies. But is all your stuff brand-new, perfectly placed, and color coordinated? In fact, it's likely that there's so much of you in your house, buyers will have a hard time seeing themselves in it. That's why a number of real estate agents and interior designers are now billing themselves as "stagers," charging $200 or more an hour to edit, enhance, renew, and rearrange your home for sale, a process known as "fluffing."

As I've written in the *Wall Street Journal*, though the concept of staging has been around for a while, it really took off in 2000, after a California real estate broker published a study showing professionally "staged" homes sold in 13.9 days, half the usual time on the market—and sold for 6.3% over list price, or four times the average markup on unstaged homes.

Even some multimillion-dollar homes need help. Stagers for high-end clients say they've had to cope with pet smells, silverfish in books, black velvet nude self-portraits, religious shrines, and, in one memorable case, a full-sized statue of C3PO placed in a foyer. One Virginia stager had to gently persuade a customer to paint over a mural of Michelangelo's David he'd created on his dining-room wall.

Here's some advice from stagers and brokers on how to give your home that almost-lived-in look:

• **Send all nonessential furniture to a self-storage warehouse.** It makes rooms look bigger, and opens up circulation paths. Leave a few pieces of high-quality artwork or antiques if you have them, but photograph or videotape them to document their worth, and make sure they're adequately insured.

• **Depersonalize.** Put away personal pictures, children's artwork, and your troll figurine collection. You want buyers to be able to project their own life dramas into your home's setting, not feel like they're trespassing on your turf.

• **Show your home's "baby pictures."** An exception to the no-photos rule is an album of the house shot in different seasons (just make sure the pictures don't include any people shots). Lay the book open on the coffee table or kitchen counter. And include descriptive captions that help buyers imagine themselves living in your home, like "In spring, 200 daffodils spring up under the pines" or "The school bus stops half a block away." If your home's builder or architect has won any design awards, or the community was included in a house or garden tour, add that information, too.

• **Leave diplomas and awards.** If you have degrees from prestigious universities, little gold statuettes named Oscar on the mantelpiece, or even awards from the Rotary Club, leave them. Agents say diplomas and awards don't raise the same territorial issues that personal photos do. But they do convey the idea that the neighborhood is full of educated, accomplished people.

• **Play to all the senses.** Sellers spend so much time obsessing over how a house looks, they forget the impression their house is making on the other senses. But these matter, too, albeit on a more subliminal level. So clean anything a buyer might touch. Polish doorknobs and doorknockers, and wipe sticky light switches. If your doorbell looks old or doesn't work, replace it.

• **Be sure the house smells good.** Clean smells like lemon furniture polish and even ammonia-based cleaners are more appealing to buyers than canned plug-in air fresheners, brokers say. If you have a bread-maker, have a loaf cooking while home shoppers visit. Buy fresh flowers for all your major rooms, as well as the master bath. Or try an old agent's trick—put a drop of vanilla extract on your fingers and dab it on all the lightbulbs before you turn them on (be sure you do this while the bulbs are cool, or they may explode).

Finally, to create a relaxing ambiance, play soft background music or a nature tape with sounds of babbling brooks and singing birds.

Shooting the House

Pictures are the most powerful tools in your sales arsenal, especially on the Internet. But most people don't spend the time, effort, or money to ensure that their photos are any better than vacation snapshots.

Builders realize the emotional impact of good photos, which is why they spend thousands of dollars having their model homes shot by professional architectural photographers. These specialized shutterbugs know how to capture a room's best profile, make grass and flowers look more lush, and capture the different nuances in the neutral colors so beloved by model home interior designers.

During my days as feature editor of *BUILDER* magazine, I used to insist that photographers accompany me to model home shoots in their own cars, so I wouldn't have to wait around for them to finish shooting. I could finish my interview with the builder in an hour or less, but I had learned the hard way that the best photographers would need at least an hour to set up their cameras, tripods, and lights in each room of the model. Once, at a remote shoot, I arrived in the same car as the photographer and wound up spending the entire afternoon sitting with him in a soggy marsh, swatting mosquitoes and waiting for the slanting sun to brighten the model's red tile roof.

How do you compete with these patient pros when you're using a $200 camera you bought at Target? The first and most important thing, says Vienna, Virginia, photographer S. A. Henderson, is to be selective. "You stand to gain more by doing less," she says. In other words, don't feel like you must show a picture of every room, especially if it's cramped, overcrowded with furniture, or is just a basic box with no special architectural details. Instead, show a picture of the front of the home and two or three major rooms, including the kitchen. Let a floor plan, plus photographs of details, like a close-up of a fireplace in the family room, or the ceiling medallion and chandelier in the foyer, convey the rest. "The idea isn't to show everything you have but to tempt people to come to your home," she says. "Leave a little to the imagination."

Here are some other tips:

• **Lighting is key.** The goal in architectural photography is to even out the overall lighting, and highlight areas that you want to emphasize. Most built-in flashes on automatic cameras are inadequate to light a room. Turning on lamps won't make up for this. In fact, they may throw off the true color of the room—incandescent bulbs will cast an orange glow, fluorescent ones a blue one. Take a course on photographic lighting, or read a book on the subject. If you can borrow or rent studio lights, do so.

• **Avoid shooting a window in the middle of the day.** Everything else in the room will look dark and dreary by comparison. Shoot early or late in the day, and don't shoot the window head-on. Put your camera on a tripod and use a long exposure to make the most of the ambient light.

(continued)

- **Remove knickknacks and clutter.** They distract the eye, and focus attention on your decor rather than the house. Remember, buyers will be clicking quickly through tiny thumbnail pictures of your house—they have to be able to "get" what they see immediately.

- **Shoot vertically as well as horizontally.** Most amateur photographers are used to shooting groups of people, which means holding the camera horizontally. But vaulted ceilings, bookcases, powder rooms, lofts, usual door frames, and many other architectural features are better captured in a vertical shot. Shoot straight on; if you tilt the camera, you'll distort the perspective and the picture may have a strange "fun house" look.

SEALING THE DEAL

Hanging up yard signs and giving staging tips is all well and good. But agents say their experience is really most valuable when it comes to negotiating the price and keeping the deal together until closing.

Richard Shell agrees with them—at least when the market is slow. Professor Shell, an attorney, teaches at the Wharton School at the University of Pennsylvania and is the author of *Bargaining for Advantage: Negotiation Strategies for Reasonable People.* He says that agents are most useful during market troughs when you have to fend off the bottom-feeders. "In a post-bubble environment, they'll earn their fees," he says.

But in boom times, you don't really need one, he says. In fact, he's sold two homes that he's owned without using an agent in rising real estate markets. The first time, in the mid-1980s, he sold a three-bedroom condo by inviting two couples who showed interest to bid against each other; by the time one

On Your Own:
Josh Horwitz's Story

Josh Horwitz got turned off to real estate agents nine years ago, when he was trying to buy a weekend getaway in quaint Waterford, Virginia.

The local market was just starting to heat up when he fell in love with a 17th-century clapboard farmhouse. Unfortunately, another buyer did, too. They began to bid against each other, but Mr. Horwitz became frustrated with the pace of the negotiations. "My agent had to call the listing agent who had to call the seller, then back the same way to me, in a big round robin," he recalls. "I started to worry I'd lose the house." So he asked his agent if he could call the seller directly and negotiate. The agent said no.

Mr. Horwitz ignored the agents, called the seller, and quickly worked out a deal for $400,000. "The agents were huffy at first, but got over it when they realized they'd still get a commission," he says.

The experience convinced Mr. Horwitz, a medical media publisher, that real estate agents "serve no useful purpose." So when it came time to put his historic five-bedroom Victorian home in Washington, D.C., on the market in March 2005, he decided to sell it himself.

To set the price, he used an appraisal that showed his house was worth $1.765 million (he decided to ask $1.799 million). He called a cleaning service to make his house shine, made some flyers, put up a sign, and paid someone $300 to put up a Web site.

About a dozen people toured the house, and the bidding began, ending at $2.1 million. It had been on the market for two days.

(continued)

After the home inspection, there was a bit more back-and-forth. The buyers convinced Mr. Horwitz to give them $10,000 for painting costs, and he convinced them to let him rent back the house for three months for $1. Mr. Horwitz had an attorney review the contract. The deal closed without a hitch.

In all, Mr. Horwitz's out-of-pocket costs to sell his home were about $1,500. "You do need a certain comfort level to do your own deal, but if you have it, I'm convinced you don't need an agent," Mr. Horwitz says. "They only stand in the way."

couple dropped out, the price was bid up $10,000 above the asking price. The second time, four years ago, he sold a six-bedroom home in Pennsylvania without even advertising. He simply told a few friends and coworkers that he wanted to sell, and got an offer within a week.

At first, he and the out-of-town buyer negotiated by e-mail. When the offers and counteroffers were $5,000 apart, Mr. Shell called him, and after a short chat, they agreed to split the difference. "In both cases, the process was painless," he says.

Negotiating usually goes smoothly if you remember two simple tricks, he says. One is to always give the other person a chance to redeem himself, even if he starts out confrontational and "acts like a jerk." Another is to show your own good faith by making concessions—but in small increments. "It's not what you offer, it's how you offer," he says.

SURVIVAL TIPS

FOR SELLERS

- **Set a realistic price.** Pricing can be particularly difficult when your market is rising or sinking rapidly. Real estate agents give you comparable sales figures, typically going back six months, but in a fast-changing market these may not mean much. Use every avenue possible to get recent sales statistics for your neighborhood, including national data providers like www.domania.com.

Pricing is tricky, since most sellers have an emotional attachment to their homes and overlook defects. So you should ask a clear-eyed and critical friend to go to nearby open houses with you to give you a critique of what those houses have that yours doesn't, and vice versa. Ask owners what sort of offers they have been getting. Hiring an appraiser to help establish a price is worth the $200 or so you'll pay for the service, since you'll then be able to show a buyer that your price isn't just pie-in-the-sky.

Naturally, you don't want to overprice your house during down markets, but you may want to avoid the temptation in boom times, too. Setting your house at market or even a little below, when everyone else is greedily overpricing, can make your house look like a bargain. That attracts more bidders, which improves your chances of getting the highest possible price.

• **Negotiate commissions.** Although real estate commissions are supposed to be negotiable, in reality, a 5% or 6% commission has become the de facto standard in most parts of the country. When I've bought and sold houses, I've been handed real estate contracts with the commission line already filled in. Brokers rarely volunteer the news to home shoppers that commissions can be bargained down.

In hot markets, it takes very little effort for agents to sell homes, and their commission levels should reflect that. But even in cool ones, you can sometimes strike a deal if you ask the agent to act as the listing agent on your old home, and the buying agent on your new one. If the agent you really want won't budge on the commission, ask him to pay for other things related to the sale, like a home warranty or inspections.

• **Make it clear that you want to see all offers.** The Code of Ethics for the National Association of Realtors requires that agents present all offers in a timely fashion, but in reality, not all agents do that. Some hold out so they can earn a bigger commission; others, so they can get an offer from one of their own clients and not have to split a commission. Let your agent know that you want to see every offer right away, even the lowball ones.

• **Give creative incentives to buyers.** A year's free maid service, lawn mowing or pool cleaning, a luxury car, a boat, or even a set of new gourmet cookware can help create excitement when the market softens. Or if interest rates rise, you can offer to pay some points so the buyer can get a lower interest rate.

• **Disclose, disclose, disclose.** In our litigious society, lack of disclosure can trip you up. About two-thirds of states mandate some sort of seller disclosure of defects, according to the National Association of Realtors. But what counts as a defect varies. Mold, radon, termites, and lead paint are considered defects just about everywhere, but other requirements are more regional—in California, for instance, you must disclose earthquake and wildfire hazards, but you don't have to in New York. In South Dakota, you must disclose if there was ever an illegal methamphetamine lab on the premises, since the residue from producing the drug known as "speed" is toxic.

To protect themselves as well as their clients, real estate agencies are adding new disclosure forms all the time. After Hurricane Charley hit Punta Gorda, Florida, and nearby Port Charlotte in 2004, the local multiple listing service added a new form requiring sellers to disclose if their properties have ever suffered any windstorm damage, and to describe the damage and any repairs. The form also asks for details about any insurance money paid for the claim.

One buyer who wrote to me in my capacity as real estate advice columnist for RealEstateJournal.com was planning to sue the seller because he'd discovered his plumbing was attached to a septic tank rather than the city sewer. One wonders why he didn't ask about this before the sale if it truly mattered to him, but in fact, some states do require you to disclose such seemingly obvious matters. Water rights, easements, and title and insurance problems also have to be disclosed in some cases. The best rule of thumb is, when in doubt, disclose.

FOR BUYERS

• **Let sellers know the reason behind your offered price.** In volatile markets, prices are all over the map. Sellers may be testing the waters with prices much higher than the market will bear, or alternatively, may set them too low, hoping to start a bidding war. If you decide to make a low offer because you think the kitchen will need a $75,000 investment in new cabinets and appliances, tell the seller that's why. Sellers are much less likely to be insulted than if they think you're just trying to take advantage of them.

• **Find out why the seller is selling.** If the owner is selling without an agent, it's simple just to ask. But when the owner is shielded by a listing agent, it's far harder—so make a few discreet inquiries with neighbors and other agents.

Motivation matters because if you can solve an owner's problem, you may be able to buy the house for less than someone who doesn't. For instance, if you find that the owner really would like to rent back the house for a few months after the closing while he looks for another house, and you're flexible about the moving date, you can put that in your offer.

• **Beware of escalation clauses.** Common in markets where there are bidding wars, these automatically trump competitors' bids up to a certain limit that you preset. But these can lock you into bidding far more than the house is worth. Unless you also have a financing contingency clause that lets you wiggle out of the deal if the house doesn't appraise for what you offered, you'll be stuck paying the difference out of your own pocket.

• **Bring in your own team.** Agents don't get paid unless the deal goes through. So they're more likely to recommend inspectors, lenders, lawyers, appraisers, and others who won't do anything to kill the deal.

That's not in your best interest. While I wouldn't assume that everyone an agent recommends is suspect, it's a good idea to check references first.

• **Find an exclusive buyer's agent.** If you use a buyer's agent, legally and ethically his loyalty lies with you, and he acts as your advocate throughout the deal. But if he's associated with a brokerage that also lists homes, there's a possibility of conflict of interest. The home that ultimately tickles your fancy might be listed by that brokerage—or even listed by the agent. State law varies as to how these cases of "dual agency" are handled, but even in the best of circumstances, and with the best of intentions, a dual agent can't be your advocate anymore. He can only be a neutral party negotiating the deal. For this reason, some states make brokerages choose whether they will represent sellers or buyers.

One way to avoid this problem is to find an agent who's a member of the National Association of Exclusive Buyer Agents (NAEBA). Members work for brokerages that don't handle listings. You can find a member by visiting the Web site www.naeba.org.

• **Negotiate builder upgrades.** If you're buying a new home, you probably won't get the builder to budge on price, because that gets him in hot water with other buyers. However, when the market is slow or when the builder wants to close out a community, you can often get a finished basement or other upgrades thrown into the deal.

But when it comes time to pick the upgrades you'll pay for, be selective. Upgrades are builders' biggest profit centers, up to 60% over cost. You can often get things cheaper if you wait until after you move in.

Generally, it's best to take builder upgrades if it would be a major hassle to have the work done after you moved in or if it involves carpentry (site-built kitchen cabinets are often superior to anything you could buy in a store). These are also things that you want to make sure will be covered by the builder's warranty. But you can get a better deal, and find more variety, if you choose decorator or easily installed items, such as wall coverings, carpets and fixtures, on your own.

• **Assume nothing.** Don't assume that the beautiful parkland behind the home you want to buy will never be developed; check with the zoning department. Don't assume that the crack in the basement is a minor defect; have an engineer look at it. Don't even assume that the school is in the same district that's on the listing sheet; call the school district. (I once visited an open house in my subdivision and saw that the elementary school on the listing sheet was one that we'd been redistricted out of five years earlier.)

Sellers and agents can be sincerely misinformed, they can be lazy, or they can be fudging the facts to make the sale. Sure, you can always sue if someone has deliberately deceived you, but who really wants the hassle and heartache? Spend some time playing reporter before you buy, and save yourself some grief.

4

Getting Smart about Home Improvements

These days, if you have the good fortune to live in a resort town or hot city, you expect to be courted by multiple bidders, even if the place hasn't been painted since the Nixon administration.

But what if you don't live in a "bubblette" town?

John Bryan lives in a 1970s-era ranch house in Cincinnati. Like most of the Midwest, it's on no one's list of hot spots. In the first quarter of 2005 prices there rose only 2.7% over the year before.

Mr. Bryan, a university professor, wants to sell his house next spring for top dollar, so he's planning to spruce it up. The laminate countertops, the ancient appliances and cabinets, and the scratched-up parquet floor, he figures, all have to go.

He budgeted about $25,000 for stylish upgrades, including

new appliances and cabinets, a charcoal solid-surface counter-top, and marble tile flooring. But when a contractor he interviewed hinted that he'd be interested in buying the house for the full $300,000 asking price, even with the Brady Bunch kitchen, Mr. Bryan began to wonder if it was worth living with the dust and disruption of remodeling—or even necessary. "Real estate agents are always saying that you need a modern kitchen to sell a house, but I have to ask—am I nuts to be doing this?"

Agents are also always saying that the only three things that matter in real estate are location, location, location. But as I said in Chapter 1, that ignores half of the equation in the space-time continuum of real estate. Timing is just as important as location, especially when it comes to deciding what—or if—to upgrade before you sell.

Like Mr. Bryan, you may have heard from real estate agents, friends, and your great aunt Sally that you have to get your home in tip-top shape before selling, and upgrade the most important rooms, the kitchen and baths. That's decent advice in slow times. In a normal market, it may or may not make sense. But when your market is peaking, even though it may not be at a double-digit, headline-inducing pace, it's a waste of money.

Three years ago, before prices in his Virginia neighborhood started to climb, airline pilot Kyle Smith spent an entire year and $8,500 sprucing up his home, refinishing floors and redoing the kitchen. He figured all the upgrades would help him fetch top dollar. But by the time he was done, homes in the area were so scarce, and prices were rising so quickly, a neighbor who had been renting a place nearby grabbed it at the $800,000 asking price, sight unseen. "My wife mentioned that we were selling our home. The neighbor said 'We'll buy it!' and only then asked how much," he says. He realized then that the market in his community had become so hot, all his effort and expense had been unnecessary.

How can you tell if the market's reaching the top? While there's no foolproof way, lines of prospective buyers or waiting lists at new-home developments, and sales occurring within days or hours of listing in existing communities are both sure signs. Putting money into a house to enhance resale value under these circumstances is foolish—particularly since would-be new-home buyers who "settle" for a resale will be more prone than most to tear out those cabinets and countertops and put in their own version of Barbie's Dream Kitchen.

Also, there's a trade-off between when you do a renovation and when you sell. If you add a bath right after you move into a house, you'll increase the home's value (particularly if adding the extra bath brings the home in line with others in your neighborhood), will amortize the cost, and, of course, will be able to use and enjoy it. But by the time you sell—if you're like most folks, the average resale window is around seven years—those brass faucets will be out, nickel will be in, and the room will look dated. You're back where you started.

On the other hand, if you hold off adding the bath until right before you sell, you'll have a bright, shiny, fashionable sales gimmick, but you probably won't get back what you invested in it.

The rule of thumb: If you're planning on moving within a year or two, don't renovate for personal taste or to impress the neighbors. This is the time to be a follower rather than a leader: Put in the colors, level of finish and materials that the neighbors already have. Appraisers say that homeowners tend to get carried away, putting in pricey cherry cabinets when oak would do, or buying a $1,000 hand-carved wet bar for a basement home theater. Gopal Ahluwalia, research director of the National

Association of Home Builders, says that every year, people remodel 2.5 million kitchens that are actually perfectly acceptable. "They do it to show off to their friends," he says.

Reining yourself in may be difficult, given the constant pressure by the media to keep up with ever-changing home fashions. The relentless status-seeking of the Boomer generation has created something of a permanent state of fix-up fever. According to Harvard University's Joint Center for Housing Studies, the home improvement industry hasn't seen a downturn since the early 1990s, when Boomers first started buying homes in bulk. Their example has set a pattern for the younger set. Though Boomers are still responsible for more than half of all remodeling expenditures, "Gen X" buyers are spending more money to redo their homes than the Boomers did when they were their age.

In 2003, the last year for which statistics were available, Americans spent $233 billion on remodeling, the Harvard study says, a figure that accounted for 40% of construction spending. About 45% was spent on projects to upgrade the home's interior, by remodeling kitchens and baths or adding room additions; 28% went to exterior replacements, including the roof, siding, windows, and doors. Amazingly, 7% of homeowners spent a sum that was more than half of their home's initial value.

Especially in the upper end, owners get so wrapped up with status seeking that they put in features that no sane buyer is ever going to underwrite. In my decade with the *Wall Street Journal*, I've interviewed people who've installed hand-embroidered wall-to-wall carpeting, crystal chandeliers, and car washes in their garages (which are big enough for dozens of cars), full-sized Broadway stages in their kids' playrooms, underwater sound systems in their swimming pools, and gold-plated gun safes in their dens.

Sure, a lot of these toys belong to celebrities, sports stars, and corporate moguls who are so rich that they don't care about resale value, and change homes almost as often as they do their Jimmy Choos. But more and more, the merely affluent are aping this sort of conspicuous consumption, and getting stuck with the bill when it's time to sell. An Iowa appraiser told me about a local businessman who'd spent $800,000 outfitting his $1 million home with a bowling alley, indoor swimming pool, and billiards room. No one wanted to pay extra for his private Disney World; indeed, no one wanted it at all. He couldn't even sell his house for the cost of the improvements.

Meanwhile, only a fifth of all of our improvement dollars each year are spent on boring, but more essential, maintenance and repair items, like loose gutters and leaky pipes. Yet those are the items that you really can't overlook. The average age of homes in America is 32 years and rising, and given the shoddy construction of most buildings these days, that's well past its prime. A study by Regis J. Sheehan and Associates found that most things begin to show signs of wear after a decade; after twenty years, just about everything is creaky. Buyers aren't stupid about this—if they see rust on the furnace or water stains on a wall, they know these things will have to be fixed. If you don't do it before you sell, they'll take it out of your wallet at the closing.

On the other hand, you don't have to be rich to make the small, arresting upgrades that do make a difference—the little memory points that can make your house the one that stands out after a weary day of home shopping.

A friend of mine embarked on a house-hunting tour in Washington, D.C., a few years ago and became enamored of a tiny octagonal window that had been added to the eaves of an early 20th-century bungalow. It hadn't cost the owner much to install, only about $300, but it brought a beam of light into what had otherwise been a dark living room, and focused the eye upward, drawing attention to the high ceilings. "No other place I saw had a charming detail like that," he told me. "It captured my imagination. I bought the window with a house attached."

HOME SWEET ATM

According to *Remodeling* magazine, when it comes to replacing worn-out things in the home, like roofing, siding—and windows, most homeowners turn to financing offered by the remodeling contractor. Upgrading the home is a different story. About two-thirds of full-scale remodeling projects are paid for in cash or with credit cards, and about 30% are financed through home-equity loans and second mortgages.

In Grandma's day, when homes only appreciated a percentage point or two a year, homeowners would rather put their hand on a hot stove burner than touch the equity in their homes, even to make it prettier. For them, equity existed for one reason—to fund their retirement. "Remember how mad Edith got at Archie Bunker in *All in the Family* when he took money out of his home to start a business?" says Leo Samet, eighty-five, a retired Silver Spring, Maryland, tax lawyer. "That's how we all felt about our homes in those days. Taking out equity was too risky."

But in the early 1990s, when mortgage rates finally fell below double digits, attitudes began to change. Several waves of refinancing followed, each bigger than the last, as folks began to look at their homes as giant ATMs that could not only shelter their Lexus, but underwrite its payments. "The living standard has been doubling with each generation," says James Glassman, managing director and senior policy strategist for J. P. Morgan Chase and Company.

The pace of withdrawals has quickened in the last few years as home prices began spiraling upward. In the late 1990s, even the cautious Mr. Samet decided to take $175,000 equity out of the home he'd lived in for more than three decades, and invest it in the stock market (fortunately, he got out before that bubble burst).

According to Goldman Sachs, homeowners took nearly $400 billion out of their homes in 2004 through cash-out refinancing, home-equity loans, and lines of credit—about twice as much as they did in 2001.

And yet, we're not really as profligate with the funds as many would believe. According to an 18-month study by the Federal Reserve beginning in January 2001, 26% of the money that's taken out of homes is used to repay debts, 11% to make stock market investments, 10% to invest in real estate or businesses, and 16% on consumer items, from furniture to vacations in France.

But the biggest percentage, 35%, of the money we take out of our homes is plowed right back in as improvements. Mr. Glassman notes that given the age of the housing stock—the oldest average age in American history—it's not really surprising that we're on a national remodeling kick. The nation's aging and sagging housing is finally getting the facelift it needs.

Most homeowners spend about 10% of the value of their home on improvements, according to Harvard's housing center. But as markets tighten and prices keep soaring, many are starting to spend more, in the nail-biting gamble that rising prices will cover the costs.

Take Duvall Hopkins and Kim Graham, Manhattanites who recently married. The newlyweds would have liked something relatively new that didn't need renovation work, but with prices so high and inventory so low, such housing is way out of reach. So instead, the couple bought a two-bedroom apartment in a 1910 building last fall in a "gentrifying" neighborhood on the Upper West Side.

The apartment was roomier than some of the newer places they saw in their price range. But it was also in sad shape, with ancient pink sinks and bathtubs, mismatched wood flooring, and a badly designed kitchen with cheap cabinets. So after buying it for $810,000, they're spending an additional $175,000 to redo the baths and update the kitchen with new steel appliances, gray marble countertops, and upgraded cabinets.

Having stretched to buy the apartment in the first place, they've financed the improvements with a five-year interest-only loan, which they realize is a big gamble—especially since, until recently, their neighborhood was considered run-down. "It's a lot of money, but we've rationalized that we'll get it back when we sell," says Ms. Hopkins. "At least we will if the bubble doesn't burst and the market dies."

These days, pulling the money out of your home is simpler than removing a nail from a wall. If you own a home, probably a day doesn't go by that a mortgage company doesn't spam your inbox, or cram your mailbox, with offers to lend you money.

Even though there are risks to these offers—the most obvious being that you can lose your home if you don't pay on time—many people take them.

It's not just because mortgage interest rates are much lower than for unsecured debts, like those owed to credit card companies; it's also because they provide tax benefits. The interest on home-equity debt on your first and second home is deductible, up to $100,000 ($50,000 if married filing separately). See IRS Publication 936 for more details.

Most lenders will let you borrow up to 80% of the current appraised value of your home; you pay it off when you sell the home. They use two different formulas to determine how much you can handle in terms of monthly payments, which they call the "debt-to-income ratio." First, they look at the percentage of your gross monthly income used for housing expenses, including mortgage principal, interest, taxes and insurance (known in the trade as PITI); and homeowner's association dues. That number shouldn't exceed 28%.

Then they look at these total housing expenses plus any recurring, long-term debt you may be carrying, such as that owed on credit cards, for car loans, and for alimony payments. That shouldn't amount to more than 36% of your gross monthly income. (For specifics on how to get the money out of your home through home-equity loans, lines of credit, and cash-out refinancing, see Chapter 2.)

But lenders certainly have a vested interest in your borrowing to the max. Don't be too quick to oblige them. You can easily overextend yourself. If you can live with a year-old Toyota rather than a new Cadillac, or can convince your son to get married in a Las Vegas wedding chapel rather than the Ritz, it beats adding to debt payments that likely will stretch out over four-and-a-half Presidential terms.

Unless you have the financial discipline to pay off these debts in a few years (and if you had that, you would have saved up the money for these things, wouldn't you?), the final sum you'll pay will be astronomical. For instance, at 6%, you'll have to pay a total of $107,919.06 to retire a $50,000 loan in 30 years, before taxes.

Save these loans for investments that can bring you at least some return, like renovations. But don't expect too much. As a rule, unless they are small and necessary to bring your home up to code or neighborhood standards, home renovations don't return what you've paid for them.

SO WHAT'S THE PAYBACK?

A "Cost versus Value" survey done by *Remodeling* magazine every year over the last sixteen years shows that on average, renovations return only between 70% and 80% of what you pay for them. (This year, the data came from a survey of 18 mid-range and upscale projects in 60 cities.) Sal Alfano, the magazine's editorial director, says it's easy to be led down the path of overspending when you're in a showroom confronted with dozens of choices of faucets or a wall of gleaming cabinets. "These days, when so many people have stretched to buy homes, they can't afford flights of fancy," he says. "Stick to the basics."

WHO DOES THE WORK?

When it comes to building professionals, there's a marked difference between new home builders and remodelers. Over the past fifteen years, home builders have consolidated at a rapid pace, and many have become Wall Street behemoths. Their analysis of market situations has reached a high level of sophistication, and they're able to respond to booms and busts with astonishing agility.

The remodeling industry, in contrast, is fragmented and small, with the top 500 contractors doing less than 4% of all jobs nationwide. Some 800,000 people in the United States, mostly self-employed contractors, do remodeling. Only about one out of four remodeling companies are big enough to have payrolls.

In boom times, all of these remodelers are more in demand than a case of Coors on Super Bowl Sunday. That puts con-

---

Remodeling 2004
"Cost versus Value Report"

MAJOR KITCHEN REMODEL

Update an outmoded 200-square-foot kitchen with new cabinets, laminate countertops, and standard double-tub stainless-steel sink with standard single-lever faucet. Include energy-efficient wall oven, cooktop, ventilation system, built-in microwave, dishwasher, and garbage disposer. Add custom lighting and new resilient floor. Finish with painted walls, trim, and ceiling. Include 30 linear feet of semicustom grade wood cabinets, including a 3-by-5-foot island.

National Average
Job cost: $42,660
Value at sale: $33,890
Cost Recouped: 79.4%

BATHROOM REMODEL

Update bathroom that's at least 25 years old. Replace all fixtures to include standard-sized tub with ceramic tile surround, toilet, solid-surface vanity counter with integral double sink, recessed medicine cabinet, ceramic tile floor, and vinyl wallpaper.

National Average
Job cost: $9,861

(continued)

Value at sale: $8,887

Cost Recouped: 90.1%

MASTER SUITE ADDITION

On a house with two or three bedrooms, add a 24-by-16-foot master bedroom suite over a crawlspace. Include walk-in closet/dressing area, whirlpool tub in ceramic tile platform, separate 3-by-4-foot ceramic tile shower, and double-bowl vanity with solid surface countertop. Bedroom floor is carpet; bath floor is ceramic tile. Paint the walls, ceiling, and trim. Add general and spot lighting and exhaust fan.

National Average

Job cost: $70,245

Value at sale: $56,257

Cost Recouped: 80.1%

FAMILY ROOM ADDITION

Add a 16-by-25-foot room on a crawl space foundation with vinyl siding and fiberglass shingle roof. Include drywall interior with batt insulation, prefinished hardwood floor, and 180 square feet of glazing, including windows, atrium-style exterior doors, and two operable skylights. Tie into existing heating and cooling.

National Average

Job cost: $52,562

Value at sale: $42,347

Cost Recouped: 80.6%

WINDOW REPLACEMENT

Replace 10 existing 3-by-5-foot double-hung windows with vinyl- or aluminum-clad, double-glazed, wood replacement windows. Wrap existing exterior trim as required to match. Don't disturb existing interior trim.

National Average

Job cost: $9,273

Value at sale: $7,839

Cost Recouped: 84.5%

ROOFING REPLACEMENT

Remove existing roofing to bare wood and dispose of properly. Install 30 squares of fiberglass asphalt shingles with new felt underlayment, galvanized drip edge, and mill-finish aluminum flashing.

National Average

Job cost: $11,376

Value at sale: $9,197

Cost Recouped: 80.8%

ATTIC BEDROOM

In a house with two or three bedrooms, convert unfinished space in attic to a 15-by-15-foot bedroom and a 5-by-7-foot shower bath. Add a 15-foot shed dormer and four new windows. Insulate and finish ceiling and walls; carpet unfinished floor. Extend existing heating and central airconditioning to new space. Retain existing stairs.

National Average

Job cost: $35,960

Value at sale: $29,725

Cost Recouped: 82.7%

BASEMENT REMODEL

Create a 20-by-30-foot entertaining area with wet bar, a 5-by-8-foot full bath, and a 12-by-12-foot auxiliary room. Exterior walls are insulated. Include five six-panel primed hardboard doors. Main

(continued)

room includes 15 recessed ceiling light fixtures, three surface-mounted light fixtures, and snap-together laminate flooring system. Bathroom includes standard white toilet, vanity with cultured marble top, resilient vinyl flooring, two-piece fiberglass shower unit, a light/fan combination, vanity light fixture, and recessed medicine cabinet. Bar area includes 10 linear feet of raised panel oak cabinets with laminate countertops, stainless-steel bar sink, single-lever bar faucet, undercounter refrigerator, and vinyl floor tile.

National Average
Job cost: $47,888
Value at sale: $36,457
Cost Recouped: 76.1%

SUNROOM ADDITION

Add a 200-square-foot sunroom to a two-story house. Form and pour footings for slab-on-grade foundation. Use exposed post-and-beam framing on interior side and extruded aluminum window frame-and-flashing system with insulated, low-E, laminated, or tempered glazing. Provide for natural ventilation using screens and ceiling fan. Insulate all non-glass areas; provide movable shades for glass area.

National Average
Job cost: $31,063
Value at sale: $22,002
Cost Recouped: 70.8%

DECK ADDITION

Add 16-by-20-foot deck using pressure-treated SYP joists supported by 4-by-4 posts set into concrete footings. Install composite deck material in a simple linear pattern. Include a built-in bench, a planter of the same decking material, and stairs. Provide a railing system made of the same composite material as the decking or a compatible vinyl system.

National Average

Job cost: $6,917

Value at sale: $6,000

Cost Recouped: 86.7%

Editor's Note: *Remodeling* magazine, published by Hanley-Wood LLC, has been publishing this report annually for more than 16 years. We'd like to thank the editors and designers at *Remodeling*, as well as the REALTORS® who contributed to bringing you this report.

Remodeling magazine's "Cost versus Value Report" © 2004 by Hanley-Wood LLC. Republication or redissemination of the report is expressly prohibited without written permission of Hanley-Wood LLC.

sumers in the maddening position of begging for appointments, waiting all day for contractors to show up, and living with shoddier work than they'd ever accept during slow seasons.

It's no wonder then, that as the market has grown hotter, more homeowners have becoming do-it-yourselfers than ever before. Forty-two percent of all home improvement projects have a do-it-yourself component, according to the Harvard's center for housing studies.

Surprisingly, do-it-yourselfers aren't just limited to the poorest part of the market—some 28% of homeowners with household incomes above $120,000 have joined the hammering class, spurred by classes at big-box stores like Home Depot and television shows like *Trading Spaces*.

Because they've had to stretch so far to get a home, some

owners are indulging in "sweat equity" because they have no other equity to draw on. Using money they got as wedding gifts, newlyweds Jeff and Laura Czaja managed to scrape up a 5% down payment on the $382,000 home in northern New Jersey they bought in April 2005, but had to finance the rest with two loans. "Prices are crazy, out of control," says Ms. Czaja.

That left nothing to fix up the World War II–era house, which was so cramped that the third bedroom had to be carved out of a walk-in closet. To finish the basement, Mr. Czaja, a scenic artist, has had to learn framing; he jollied a friend's father into helping with electrical work. There was simply no other way to get the work done, given how expensive even modest homes have become in suburbs within commuting distance of New York City, where Ms. Czaja works.

DO YOU REALLY NEED THOSE GRANITE COUNTERTOPS?

Okay, say your market has finally cooled, and the bidding wars have stopped. In fact, let's assume that it's cooled to the point where houses are sitting on the market for several months, and buyers are offering prices below the 10% discount that is normal in normal times.

You realize you're not only going to have to fix obvious defects, like that big dent in the garage wall you made the first day you drove home the Hummer; you're going to have to upgrade your home's look to grab buyer's attention. What should you do?

You pick up a copy of a shelter magazine and see that most of the homes have granite countertops, stainless steel appliances, big spa tubs, marble showers, and gleaming hardwood floors. Do you need all those things, too?

Actually, no. The simple reason is, that though these things are desirable, they have become such fashion clichés that they're practically invisible to home shoppers. On the other hand, if every home in your neighborhood has granite counter-tops, laminate is going to seem chintzy and out of place.

That doesn't mean that you need to spring for the granite, which costs between $30 and $80 per square foot, uninstalled. Rather, this is the time for selective chic.

Start reading shelter magazines in a different way. Look for creative uses of less expensive materials and finishes—though you have to be careful, of course, not to do something that's so out of character with the style of your house it becomes an eye-sore (steel roping found on bridges looks striking when used as stair balusters in a contemporary house, but ridiculous in a colonial).

You don't have to be totally beige and boring, despite what real estate agents might say. For instance, concrete can be used for both countertops and floors at a cost of less than $1 a square foot. It can be stained any color and inlaid with anything from seashells to computer chips to give it a distinctive look. And it's popular with the *Architectural Digest* set. One wealthy woman who furnished her Colorado vacation house in a southwestern style asked the contractor to leave a small cube indentation in her kitchen island countertops, covered with a square of clear plastic. She put tiny pots, people and ladders in the cube "room," so it looked like a pueblo scene. Though the kitchen had plenty of flashy accoutrements, from a Sub-Zero fridge to a Viking range, this homely tableau became the room's focal point, the one detail that guests inevitably remembered.

Very often, it's the small details that stick in the imagination of buyers, not the big upgrades. Because of this, it may not make sense to replace your kitchen cabinets if they're func-tional—replacing, refinishing, or even just painting the cabinet doors may be enough. Spend the money instead on top-grade hardware. Some new knobs and pulls come in eye-catching "sculptural" shapes that look like tiny knives, forks and spoons, twigs, or stick people.

Also, think of ways to make simple changes that cure your home's most challenging problems, like the clever owner who put in a tiny window high in the eaves that charmed my architect friend. Since you've probably gotten used to your home's defects—the things that home shoppers will inevitably hone in on—invite your most critical friend over for coffee and ask her to point them out to you. You'll make her day.

SAVVY SUBSTITUTES

As I've written in the *Wall Street Journal,* here are some substitutions for pricey items that will make a good impression:

Instead of:	Cost:	Use:	Cost:
Whirlpool tub	$1,000–$25,000	Multiple showerheads	$100–$2,500

Because: Most people take showers rather than baths, and many homeowners who already have a spa tub find they use it only a few times a year. As the population ages, more people will find it difficult to climb into a tub. Some multiple showerhead systems come as units that attach at the old showerhead and can be installed by the klutziest homeowner ever to own a wrench.

Instead of:	Cost:	Use:	Cost:
Solid cherry entry door with two sidelites	$2,100	Fiberglass entry with two sidelights	$600

Because: Like any wood, cherry warps and shrinks over time, can be tasty to termites, and needs to be refinished after a few seasons in the sun. Inert fiberglass doesn't have any of these problems. "I can't tell some of the latest models from the real thing, even close up," says Sal Alfano, the editorial director of *Remodeling* magazine.

Instead of:	Cost:	Use:	Cost:
Hardwood floors	$5 per square foot	Laminate floors	$2.60 per square foot

Because: Laminates, which are really photographs of wood, marble, and other upscale materials, have become incredibly realistic-looking in the past few years. Although they can't be refinished like wood can, they can be damp-mopped, which is one reason why some buyers actually prefer them.

Instead of:	Cost:	Use:	Cost:
Wood or gas fireplace	$3,000	Electric fireplace	$1,500

Because: Electric fireplaces have become much more realistic-looking. Also, because they don't have to be vented like wood or gas fireplaces, they can be put in any room.

Instead of:	Cost:	Use:	Cost:
Low-Flow Toilet	$300	Your old toilet	Free

Because: Manufacturers swear that wider traps and better flushing mechanisms have made low-flow toilets more effective, and studies show that they are, but buyers still hate them. By law, you have to put one in if you add a bath, and it *is* the eco-friendly thing to do. But if you're just upgrading an existing bath and have the old 3.5-gallon model, you can reinstall it.

WHAT BUILDERS ARE DOING

Many people, quite rightly, snoop through their neighbors' houses when they're up for sale, trying to get decorating ideas and a handle on the competition. But sometimes they forget to look at new homes in their area, too. That's a mistake, since buyers often look at new homes first as they begin to shop, and these are what set the standards in their minds.

Although it's rarely practical to try to mimic everything that's in a model, unless you're tearing down your old house and rebuilding from scratch, you should pay attention to what builders are pushing. After all, they have done tons of market research and work with focus groups on what buyers in your area want before ever turning a shovelful of dirt.

The idea isn't to reproduce what builders are doing, because you simply can't win that war from a financial standpoint. Builders buy their granite countertops in bulk and get discounts on installation because they put in dozens in one day; you're going to have to pay retail.

Rather, you should tour models to get an idea what sort of lifestyle dream they are weaving, and then try to reproduce that *feeling* in your own home.

For instance, it may be impossible to put nine-foot ceilings in your new kitchen, and you won't get your money back if you do figure out a way (see the "Cost versus Value Report"). But you should understand what buyers like about this feature—in this case, the addition of more light, and a feeling of spaciousness—and do things that boost those qualities in your home. If your market is slow and you have to spring for a major redo, or you plan to live in your home for a few years, it could be as expensive as adding a few big bay windows. If homes are selling quickly, you might just want to remove some clutter, paint rooms a lighter shade, and up the wattage of your lightbulbs.

Keep in mind that many builders are also trying to make their homes more accessible to all segments of the population by widening doorways, varying counter heights in kitchens and baths (so they'll be usable by the short and tall, young and old, and people in wheelchairs), installing lever doorknobs that are easier for people with arthritis to open, and mounting appliances in cabinets so you don't have to stoop to use them. Given that 37.5 million people, or 14% of the population who don't live in institutions, have at least one disability, and that the country in general is getting older and creakier, it makes sense to add accessible features when you remodel, too.

Meanwhile, on the outside, older homes have an automatic curb-appeal advantage over newer ones because the landscaping is mature, while new homes are surrounded by twiglets. But since older homes are sometimes smothered by overgrown bushes and trees, it actually may make more sense to have some plants taken out rather than put in, especially if they're blocking light and views. While beds of flowers create curb appeal at low cost, skip the more expensive features like fountains, pergolas, and especially, swimming pools and spas, which many families rightly consider a liability. Studies show that these items return less than a third of their cost.

Every year, the National Association of Home Builders does a study of several thousand consumers to find out what they want. Below are some highlights from their latest study. Bear in mind that these are national numbers; what buyers want may be a little different in your area:

- The top kitchen features homeowners want are a walk-in pantry (84%), island work area (77%), special-use storage (62%), and built-in microwave (62%).
- Thirty-seven percent said they wanted their kitchens visually open to the family room, with a half wall; 34% want the wall to come down, leaving the two rooms completely open.
- Most-sought-after bathroom features were a linen closet (91%), exhaust fan (88%), and separate shower enclosure (78%).
- Younger households prefer their washer and dryer to be located near the bedroom; older households prefer them near the kitchen.
- Brick was preferred by 44% of respondents for the front exterior wall material.
- Higher-end buyers wanted a "flex," or bonus room, above a three-car garage.
- Asked to choose between more space in the master bedroom and less in the master bath or the opposite, 69% chose more bedroom space.
- Asked to choose between a bigger house with fewer amenities, or a smaller house with more, 63% would choose the smaller home.

THE STUFF YOU CAN'T IGNORE

We shouldn't ignore fixing items like the light switches that make a little *pftzzzz* sound every time we turn them on, or the sewer drain so clogged with tree roots we've knitted a cozy for the plunger. And yet we do, regularly. According to a 2003 Yankelovich survey, about a quarter of Americans didn't plan to spend any money on repairs in the previous year.

That's a big mistake. Sure, it's a lot more fun to buy a pretty crystal vase than to spend $50 to have the furnace tuned, but what's more important? According to Marshall and Swift, a building cost data provider based in Los Angeles, there are nine critical systems or appliances in a house, and they are just itching to break—in fact, the likelihood that one of them will fail in any given year is 68%. They are: air-conditioning, oven, refrigerator, dishwasher, water heater, washer, furnace, garage door opener, and plumbing. Just about every house is a money pit, since these critical systems wear out. Their average life span is 13 years; to replace any one of them costs, on average, about $1,100.

According to a recent survey done for American Home Shield by Ipsos U.S. Express, the percentage of homeowners who said they had to repair an item one or more times within the past year is as follows:

- Oven/range 32%
- Dishwasher 28%
- Refrigerator 34%
- HVAC (heating, ventilation, and air-conditioning) 16%
- Plumbing 47%
- Electrical 25%
- Water Heater 38%
- Furnace 39%

Buyers are much more likely to look at the condition of your refrigerator than they are to inspect your pipes, of course, but this doesn't mean that they aren't both critically important especially should one of them fail right after a new owner moves in. (Or at an even more inopportune time—my husband and I once closed on a house in a rainstorm, and the sump pump failed at exactly the moment we were signing the closing papers, flooding the basement.)

It's also an excellent reason to buy a seller's home warranty policy, which costs between $300 and $500 and can be purchased online or through real estate agents. Companies providing this service include Home Warranty of America, HMS National, and Total Protect. Although coverage by these policies is limited to the critical home systems, and riders often have to be added to cover swimming pools and other features, it's a useful sales tool. But beware: Most of these policies have at least $35 deductibles, only last a year, and have renewal fees that are often more expensive than the policy's original cost. Also, like medical insurers, most companies won't pay for "preexisting" conditions.

SURVIVAL SUMMARY

- Don't renovate when it's clear from your research that home values are on the rise where you live.
- If you plan on moving in a year or two, renovate only to neighborhood standards.
- Don't overextend yourself on major home improvements, and don't expect to get back everything that you paid for them.
- Concentrate on creating memorable focal points with inexpensive upgrades.
- Think of new homes, as well as existing ones, as competition for buyers.
- In boom times when labor is scarce, expect to be a do-it-yourselfer.
- Budget for repair and maintenance items.
- Bring everything in your house up to code.
- To sell your house faster, offer a home warranty.

Keeping Up the House

SHOULD YOU UPGRADE OR IMPROVE BEFORE YOU MOVE?

Yes, If . . .

- Something in your house is not up to code, especially if it involves the electrical system (and while you're at it, upgrade the wiring and add more outlets so your home will be more computer-friendly). Especially, check that outlets near sources of water, like sinks and baths, have ground-fault interrupters.

- Cracks in a foundation wall or floor are more than a quarter inch across.

- Fireplaces don't have combustion vents that draw air from outside, and a spark arrestor at the top of the chimney.

- Pipes are leaking or rusty. (Replace any drywall damaged by water, too—even if buyers don't notice an old leak, you can be sure the home inspector will.)

- Tests show your home has radon, or other environmentally sensitive problems like damaged popcorn ceilings that are flaking off asbestos fibers.

- Insulation isn't up to snuff. The Department of Energy's Web site has a useful calculator that helps you determine how much insulation is necessary for a new or existing home, depending on Zip code. (Also, put foam backers behind light switches and electrical outlets to prevent heat from escaping.)

- Carpets are more than five years old, or have rips, tears, and permanent stains.

(continued)

- Decks are more than a decade old and are starting to splinter.
- Gutters are loose or hanging.
- Other homes in the neighborhood have been remodeled extensively and recently.

No, If . . .

- The project doesn't bring your home up to neighborhood standards. For instance, if your home has three bedrooms and all the others in your community have four, don't waste your money on a kitchen redo.
- An addition would make your home too large for the neighborhood.
- On a per-square-foot basis, remodeling costs are substantially higher in your area than new construction.
- The project would boost your home's worth above neighborhood values.
- The improvement could create safety concerns, especially for families with children—examples are swimming pools, hot tubs, ponds, fountains, and waterfalls.

INEXPENSIVE UPGRADES
THAT MAKE A DIFFERENCE

- Upgraded light sconces by the front door and in the entry hallway
- Thick carpet pad under a mid-priced carpet (it feels as luxurious as a high-priced carpet with a lower-grade pad)
- Safety features that appeal to families with young children, like antiscald devices on the shower and plastic "push" locks on cabinet doors
- Noise-reducing features that hush your house, like laminated glass windows, solid-core doors, and insulated washers and dishwashers

- Window-sash screws in first-floor windows that discourage burglars
- Painting the front door a bright color that contrasts with shutters or trim
- New hardware, kickplate, and knocker for the front entry door
- New kitchen hardware
- Pots of flowers or small evergreens framing the front door
- New window screens replacing any ripped ones

5

The Flip Side: Investing without Losing Your Shirt

Today, it's hard to open up a newspaper without seeing an ad from a real estate guru blaring easy-money schemes that encourage you to take all the equity in your home and use it to control lots of other homes.

And we've become highly leveraged believers. Last year, homeowners extracted $750 billion of home equity. SRI Consulting Business Intelligence, a Menlo Park, California, research firm, found that nearly 2.2 million households used their home equity to buy more property last year, compared with about 1 million a decade earlier.

How can you resist when the high rollers are in the game for big stakes? Like Donald Trump, who is putting one of his apprentices in charge of the renovation of a $41.3 million, 11-bedroom oceanfront home he just bought in Palm Beach, which he then plans to flip for millions in profit.

Meanwhile, Trump wannabes are listening to the same siren song. The number of real estate investor clubs has tripled over the past three years, according to the National Real Estate Investors Association, a trade group started in 1993. Even *Playboy*'s twenty-three-year-old May 2005 "Playmate of the Month" announced in the magazine that she plans a new career investing in real estate.

But the average person just doesn't have the time or expertise to beat the professionals at this game, who typically look for bedraggled properties in working-class parts of town, not oceanfront mansions. Plus, because thousands of amateurs have been suckered into get-rich-quick schemes and are all following the same precepts, you'll have plenty of competition for any home where there's a whiff of distress, divorce, or other sign that a bargain can be had.

According to the National Association of Realtors, about a quarter of the homes in the country are currently being bought as investments—up from a historical norm of around 5% or 6%. In hot markets like Las Vegas, the proportion is even higher. The fact that investors are propping up today's hot housing market is a cause for concern, according to Gopal Ahluwalia, director of research for the National Association of Home Builders. Unlike people who are buying for shelter, investors don't need to buy, and are the first to leave a market when they sense it is cooling. A mass exodus of investors could even collapse a market where they had heavy stakes. "It could be very worrisome," he says.

Investors make their money on a property in one of three ways: by renovating it and increasing its value, by renting it out, or by holding it a short time, and then "flipping" it to a new buyer.

The first method is most common in a slow market, when sellers need to add value to a property to make it attractive; the second way is most common in a normal market, where prices are growing at a steady pace, but owners need to hold on to the property awhile to realize a profit. Both of these are labor-intensive activities, and incur costs. But they're also relatively low on risk.

Flipping is another story. It's popular when markets are manic, with short supply and rapidly rising prices. Flippers stand to make fortunes when prices rise, as long as they sell quickly before the peak (a flipper recently pocketed $900,000 when he sold a New York apartment to singer Billy Joel). Some areas are currently awash with them—in southwest Florida, for example, McCabe Research estimates that speculators already have purchased up to 60% of the 60,000 new homes and condos scheduled to be completed by 2007.

Two new television programs devoted to the subject debuted in the summer of 2005. *Property Ladder,* on the TLC channel, plays to the new flipper demographic as, the company's program notes say, "novice real estate developers attempt to renovate properties considered 'diamonds in the rough' and re-sell them for a lucrative profit." Meanwhile, *Flip That House,* on the Discovery Channel, "tells the real stories of people gutsy enough to buy a fixer-upper, gambling that they can 'flip' that home from wannabe to where-to-be," according to the show's promotional materials.

Speculating is so rampant, some purchasers are buying their homes sight unseen. Realtybid.com, a three-year-old on-line real-estate auction house, says about 10% of the homes they feature sell this way.

But speculators can be burned, too. One Huntington Beach, California, contractor flipped 43 houses during the boom between 1988 and 1993. While prices were going up, he made a bundle—and then lost his shirt when the market suddenly fell flat. Though the market in Orange County is currently white-hot, he expects another fall is coming soon. "I don't own anything now," he says.

A common tactic for flippers is to buy homes in the preconstruction stage and then resell the contract for a profit. The practice worries many home builders, who then wind up competing with the flippers for customers. Many are starting to put clauses in their contracts to limit the practice. According to a recent survey by the National Association of Home Builders, 64% of builders currently won't let buyers sell the home or contract before closing, and 82% said they would sell only to buyers who promised to occupy the homes.

Professional investors who flip properties will abandon a market as soon as they sense it's in trouble; amateurs will be caught unaware as prices collapse, and will be most in danger of foreclosure. Consequently, areas like Las Vegas, Orange County, California, and southern Florida, where a lot of flipping has occurred, are among "the shakiest in the country," says Arlington, Virginia, housing economist John Tuccillo.

What's worse, the quick riches that can be had in a white-hot market attract crooked real estate agents, appraisers, and investors who collude to pump up the price of a property to unrealistic levels, get maximum financing, and then default on the loan. The lender can't sell the house for the last sales price; if this happens often enough, the whole market is flooded with foreclosures and prices suffer. The Federal Bureau of Investigation in 2004 had three times as many reports of such suspicious activity (17,127) as it had the year before. To short-circuit such predatory schemes, some government agencies and lenders are trying to put controls on fast sales. For instance, the Federal Housing Administration won't issue mortgage insurance, and U.S. Bank won't fund loans, for any sales that happen within 90 days of purchase.

Of course, we're not just speculating on pure investment properties. One out of every 10 properties being bought in this country today is a vacation home. Many vacation homes fall into a gray area between a residence and an investment because they're used at least part of the time as a rental. Sales of vacation homes have soared over the last few years, and prices are up 21%, according to Cambridge, Massachusetts, research firm FISERV/CSW—about twice the rate of homes overall.

But owning a vacation home is often no vacation. New owners have the hassles of having to find everything from carpenters to replace a rotting back porch to house sitters who will keep an eye on the place while they're away. Doing taxes will relieve you of another fistful or two of hair when April rolls around.

Not to mention the strain of landlording if you've never done it before: Even folks with upscale properties that I've interviewed over the years have had to deal with tenants who've held open-house parties, built wood fires in gas fireplaces, snuck in unauthorized roommates, and flooded sewer fields with a garden house. One even demanded that an owner drive from Manhattan to the Hamptons to replace a burned-out lightbulb.

New York luxury real estate broker Barbara Corcoran says new landlords usually underestimate how much it will cost to market, furnish, and maintain their homes and wind up giving away too much in negotiations. Even she's fallen into that trap, once accepting her tenant's security deposit as a last rent payment. "The apartment was trashed and the air-conditioner missing when he left," she says.

Top Vacation-Home Markets

Below are places with the biggest five-year gains in housing prices through the fourth quarter of 2004 among Zip codes with 500 or more vacant seasonal homes and a median price of $350,000 or more.

Town/City	Zip Code	Vacant Seasonal Housing Units*	Median Price**	Price Change, 5 Years	Price Change, 2004
Oceanside, CA	92054	1,288	$509,000	161.6%	28.3%
Morro Bay, CA	93442	1,014	$542,000	150.5%	22.1%
Brigantine, NJ	08203	3,134	$358,500	149.9%	15.2%
Oxnard, CA	93035	906	$580,000	149.2%	28.4%
Paso Robles, CA	93446	711	$415,000	148.0%	20.3%
Beach Haven, NJ	08008	11,569	$687,500	146.7%	18%
Cambria, CA	93428	743	$577,500	145.0%	30.7%
La Quinta, CA	92253	2,563	$416,500	143.0%	42.9%
Newport, RI	02840	858	$372,000	141.9%	17.7%
Laguna Beach, CA	92651	1,079	$1,450,000	137.8%	24.7%
Sea Isle City, NJ	08243	4,864	$699,000	136.0%	21.9%
Pompano Beach, FL	33062	6,254	$355,000	134.9%	27.1%
Dana Point, CA	92629	599	$829,000	132.8%	22.1%
Ocean City, NJ	08226	11,440	$650,000	132.4%	19.3%
Newport Beach, CA	92663	734	$1,667,000	131.8%	22.7%
St. Petersburg, FL	33706	3,040	$405,000	129.5%	28.8%
North Palm Beach, FL	33408	1,522	$360,000	126.6%	28.9%
Malibu, CA	90265	651	$1,700,000	126.1%	25.6%
Carmel, CA	93923	825	$970,000	125.4%	29.2%
Lavallette, NJ	08735	3,119	$557,500	124.8%	15.6%
Pebble Beach, CA	93953	508	$1,255,000	122.2%	27.8%
Carlsbad, CA	92009	565	$800,500	122.0%	23.6%
Forestville, CA	95436	502	$350,000	121.9%	21.1%
Margate City, NJ	08402	2,553	$549,000	121.9%	18.5%
Sayville, NY	11782	1,759	$435,000	117.7%	10.8%
Spring Lake, NJ	07762	696	$523,000	114.7%	15.7%
Miami, FL	33129	832	$410,000	114.5%	23.7%

Manasquan, NJ	08736	754	$545,000	114.2%	13.5%
West Palm Beach, FL	33414	998	$350,000	111.8%	28.3%
Mattapoisett, MA	02739	538	$353,500	110.7%	11.1%
Jupiter, FL	33477	2,855	$396,000	110.6%	27.2%
Napa, CA	94558	863	$555,000	110.1%	15.1%
Watsonville, CA	95076	977	$544,000	110.0%	24.6%
Belmar, NJ	07719	1,111	$366,500	108.3%	11.7%
Sonoma, CA	95476	503	$622,000	108.1%	19.1%
Westport, MA	02790	599	$395,000	107.5%	9.9%
Hull, MA	02045	687	$361,500	104.1%	16.5%
Boca Raton, FL	33431	911	$400,000	102.7%	22%
Long Beach, NY	11561	842	$475,000	99.5%	14%
Palm Beach Gardens, FL	33418	1,525	$362,500	98.5%	27.5%
Miami, FL	33180	3,257	$350,000	95.1%	25.6%
Marshfield, MA	02050	1,241	$414,000	83.9%	10.9%
Gloucester, MA	01930	961	$365,000	78.9%	9.5%
Santa Cruz, CA	95062	729	$644,000	78.2%	16%
Rockport, MA	01966	550	$447,500	77.6%	11.4%
Aptos, CA	95003	1,239	$680,000	75.3%	15.1%
Old Saybrook, CT	06475	900	$366,000	70.2%	11.6%
Madison, CT	06443	702	$462,000	70.0%	10%
Scottsdale, AZ	85255	808	$565,000	69.4%	24.5%
Santa Cruz, CA	95060	577	$690,000	68.9%	14.6%
Scottsdale, AZ	85260	667	$360,000	64.8%	25.1%
Scottsdale, AZ	85258	2,117	$380,000	64.1%	21.7%
Fountain Hills, AZ	85268	1,234	$372,000	59.9%	26%
Scottsdale, AZ	85262	1,672	$615,000	50.2%	20.4%
Total				**114.4%**	**21.4%**

Source: FISERV/CSW

*Not occupied by an owner as his or her primary residence.

**As of the fourth quarter of 2004.

THE INVESTOR TEST

There are three kinds of real estate investors: rehabbers, land-lords, and flippers. Do you have the right stuff to make it in one or more of these roles? Ask yourself the questions below:

To Be a Rehabber

1 Do you know an honest and thorough inspector who will be able to estimate what needs to be fixed in terms of major systems like plumbing, electrical and heating, ventilation and air-conditioning systems?

2 Can you do professional-level renovation work, or do you have a team assembled who can do it for you?

3 Have you the time and skill to obtain building and architectural plans, supervise subcontractors, and handle problems as they crop up?

4 Will the improvements you have planned for the property bring you at least twice what you paid for them?

5 Are you willing to take on properties in junk- and crime-ridden neighborhoods that might scare people?

6 Are you willing to take on an abandoned or partially completed building?

7 Do you have a good eye for what can be done to improve a property cosmetically?

8 Are you up-to-date on design trends, especially in kitchens and baths?

9 Are you planning to live in the house during the renovation? What does your spouse think about this arrangement?

10 Can you find tenants willing to live in the unit while it's being rehabbed, perhaps for a below-market rent?

To Be a Landlord

1 According to the National Association of Realtors, second homeowners earn more than 80% more than the typical American household. Do you fit the financial profile of a typical owner of a second home?

2 Are you buying something you'll live in some of the time, or in the case of a duplex or multifamily dwelling, all of the time? How will this affect your lifestyle?

3 If you aren't going to live in the unit, who will handle property management and maintenance for you?

4 Can you cover the cost of the loan, taxes, and insurance; the settlement costs; utilities; repairs; and replacement of damaged or worn items even if your unit is vacant for half of the year—or longer?

5 Can you handle the cost of unexpected disasters—a water heater that dies and floods the downstairs unit, a hurricane that blows off the roof and ruins all of your furniture?

6 Have you budgeted for improvements and upgrades?

7 Have you a contract that's been vetted by a good local lawyer?

8 Are you prepared to go through a long and frustrating eviction process if a tenant doesn't pay?

To Be a Flipper

1 Are you willing to make installment sales, offer wrap-around mortgages, or offer other forms of seller financing to sell a home?

2 Do you have sources of cash besides banks to fund your purchases?

3 Can you acquire your target home for significantly less than other homes in the neighborhood?

4 Do you have contacts with lenders, real estate agents, and others who can alert you to bargain properties before they go on the market?

5 Are you aware of new-home projects where you can buy in the preconstruction phase and then sell for a profit to other buyers?

6 Are you in tune enough with local market conditions to get out before prices fall?

INVEST WITH THE BEST

Okay, don't say I didn't warn you—as prices continue to balloon around the country, it's getting mighty late in the game to start flipping houses. "You have to buy low and sell high, and you can't do that on the tail end of a cycle," says Peter Miller, president of Restore Media LLC, a Washington, D.C., publisher of remodeling and shelter magazines.

He speaks from both personal and professional experience. In 1983, as the Washington, D.C., market was just beginning to rebound from a slump, Mr. Miller came home one day and found his next-door neighbor crying. She told him the owner of the house she was renting planned to sell it, and she was afraid she'd be kicked out. So Mr. Miller called the owner and he and a partner bought the house before it even went on the market— for about $60,000 less than what it was worth.

The partner arranged for some architecture students to paint and to upgrade hardware and light fixtures. "We just did the flash factors," Mr. Miller said. Meanwhile, the tenant decided she didn't want to keep renting after all, so Mr. Miller and his partner sold the place about six months after they bought it, netting about twice what they paid for it. As the market heated even more, the property was flipped two more times, with each new owner adding more space and features to try to increase the property's value—one even added a second floor. Neither, however, doubled their money like Mr. Miller and his partner did with just cosmetic improvements. The others were simply too late to the party.

So what if you still want to invest in real estate, but think it's just too late in the cycle to buy and flip? You can still make money, but you need more skill in finding genuine bargains, arranging financing, and locating buyers. There are numerous good books on the subject—for a list, see the notes for this chapter at the end of this book—but you should also consult knowledgeable local sources, including real estate brokers, lenders, and appraisers. Here, also, are some tips:

• **Avoid properties that are overfinanced.** With so many people putting as little down as possible and financing the rest with shaky loans, this is going to be tough to do over the next few years. But it's probably the most important point to keep in mind. Sellers who are deep in hock have no wiggle room on the price. Even if they are in distress due to delinquency, divorce, or some other problem, and are in a declining market, they aren't going to sell you a home for less than they owe on their loan.

• **Look for homes that are privately financed.** You may be able to buy back the note at a discount if the note holder needs cash now or in the near future. (Good candidates are note holders who are going through a divorce, have children in college, or want cash to make other investments.)

- **Pick a location that will boost your cash flow.** If you're going to live in the property full- or part-time, pick an attractive location—though you may have to give up visiting during the prime season to maximize rents. If you aren't going to live there, you'll probably find that the best cash flow is to be found in the most run-down parts of town.

- **Roll improvement costs into your primary loan.** This will help maximize your cash flow.

- **Look for alternative sources of cash.** You can go to a traditional lender like a bank, of course, but if rates go up, that eats into your profits. Not to mention the onerous paperwork. Professional investors have other sources of cash for their down payments and settlement costs, which come from such sources as rental income, carry-back notes, or down payments on properties they've sold, or "hard money" (private) lenders, who invest their own funds in such deals. You can even sell some things you don't want or need, like old kayaks and sofas, to come up with cash.

- **Raid your IRA.** Many people overlook a source of cash that's right under their noses—their individual retirement accounts. A self-directed individual IRA or employer-based self-directed retirement plan, like a 401(k), SEP or profit-sharing plan, can all be invested in real estate, as long as it is overseen by a third-party IRA administrator. You don't have to buy homes with the money, either; you can also use the money to purchase discounted notes or income streams from notes, tax lien certificates, mortgages or deeds of trust, or commercial real estate. There are some caveats, however:

Neither you nor any of your family members may have ever owned the property before and the purchase must be an investment only, not your personal home or the location of your business. Also, as with any other IRA, you can't pull out the money before your retirement age without incurring a withdrawal penalty—but whatever you earn is tax-deferred until you retire, presumably at a lower income level than you have now.

• **Buy before subdivision approval.** In a number of states, you can make a reservation on a property for a few thousand dollars but can't complete the sale before the development has received local and state approval. If the project sells out in a rising market, you can sell your reservation to someone else for a profit.

This was, of course, how quick fortunes were made during the big Florida real estate rush in the 1920s—and though builders are trying to crack down on the practice, many are trying to do the same thing today in blistering markets like Miami. Some units in waterfront projects have changed hands two or three times before the sales office opened to the public.

• **Look for properties with high rent-to-value ratios.** The best investments produce good cash flow streams, regardless of appreciation. Try to find properties where the rent-to-total-value ratio is 1.5 or better. In other words, if a property costs $200,000, you'll want to be able to collect $3,000 a month in rent. Obviously, getting these sorts of returns is tough unless it's a duplex or multifamily property, or in a resort area where you can collect hefty seasonal rents.

• **Hold properties in land trusts.** Each time you acquire a property, deed it into a separate land trust, managed by a trustee of your choice but directed by you. It will cost you a small recording fee. But it will protect you financially should a disgruntled tenant or subcontractor win a judgment against you in court. Setting up a land trust is generally cheaper than starting a corporation, which is another way to protect your personal assets. If you flip properties, however, it may be to your advantage to set up a corporation to avoid the tax consequences of being classified as a dealer (see "A Word on Taxes," on page 132).

VACATION HOME NATION

If you're buying a home primarily for your own use, or as a potential retirement residence, it doesn't really matter what the local real estate market does. So go ahead and buy if you feel like it. And pull out those volleyball nets, dust off the Adirondack chairs, and grill my hamburger medium-rare, please.

But if you're buying one because you want to keep up with Courteney Cox, your hairdresser, and your Uncle Bill, or because you're afraid the real estate train is leaving you in the station, think again.

Just because Americans bought a little more than a million vacation homes last year doesn't mean you have to, or should. While coastal vacation home markets are among those that have appreciated the fastest over the last five years, they're also the most vulnerable to a downturn, according to Cambridge, Massachusetts, economist David Stiff. "They're probably the most vulnerable to price declines of any markets in the country," he says.

And when should you just say no? When you can't afford the payments without pain, or don't have the time or skill to do what it takes to rent out your home and ensure a positive cash flow.

It may take more than a little intestinal fortitude to buck the trend, but there are alternatives to buying that beach bungalow. You can always rent a summer place, of course, or you could try some of the more resourceful solutions below:

• **Time Shares.** When time shares first emerged in the early 1960s, they were something only the most naive investors would buy. Once you plunked down your money, you were stuck with a week in April at Disney World forever, even after your kids had headed off to graduate school.

But much has changed for the better in the time-share industry, especially since big players like Marriott, Hilton, Ramada, Fairfield Resorts, and Westin have gotten into it. In 1975, there were only about 45 places to find time shares in America, plus a few more places in Europe; now there are more than 4,000 resorts worldwide. Nor are you limited just to fixed weeks; you can get "floating" weeks or points that allow you to vary your vacation time and trade it for weeks at other resorts.

It can be a little tricky to exchange your week for someone else's, however, because you must find a unit and week of comparable value first (exchange companies color-code weeks, depending on desirability, with red generally the most desirable and blue the least). And if you back out of the exchange, some companies make you pay a cancellation penalty.

You can buy either an equity or nonequity (right-to-use) time share. Equity ownership gives the same tax benefits as any other head of home ownership, and these can be bought or sold freely; there may be resale or rental limitations on nonequity ownership, which expires after a certain number of years.

Although time shares don't appreciate like other real estate—in fact, they can sell for less than half of their purchase price—thanks to eBay and numerous other Web ad venues, plus the efforts of specialized time-share brokers, at least there's now a resale market for them.

Upscale resorts have developed some twists on the time-share concept. One, *fractional ownership*, covers not just a week, but longer shared time periods, at prices in the six digits rather than the low five digits usually charged for regular time-shares. They usually hold their value better than time shares because they're in high-end communities with swanky amenities where outright ownership would cost millions. And appreciation rates are generally the same as they are for outright ownership. Former National Football League quarterback and Hall of Famer Joe Montana recently bought a one-twelfth interest of a villa at Pronghorn, a luxury golf community in Bend, Oregon. One-twelfth to one-quarter ownership shares at the community range from $140,000 to $425,000.

Another variation is called a *private vacation club*. Members don't own a piece of a specific property, but rather the right to use different upscale properties in various locales. At the Portofino Club, for instance, a club with resorts in 25 different cities, members stay at million-dollar homes complete with 300-thread-count sheets, fresh flowers, and stocked pantries. Concierges arrange for everything from personal chefs to spa appointments. But for the pampering, members pay $250,000 (80% refundable) to join, with

$15,500 annual dues. Vacation club owners get a wider choice of vacation spots than fractional owners, but don't accrue equity.

• **Condo-Hotels.** Also known as "condotels," these properties allow you to buy a luxury hotel room, and all the perks that go along with it, without the usual hassles of owning and managing a property. When you are not using the room, it goes into a rental program managed by the developer. Stays usually can't exceed six months. About three years ago, WCI Communities, based in Bonita Springs, Florida, started building its version of condo-hotels, which it calls "resort residences," in some of its upscale condo communities. The company is selling them as fast as they go on the market. At the Resort at Singer Island, for instance, the residences come fully furnished down to the 42-inch LCD TVs and Bose stereo system, and share many of the amenities with the regular condo owners, including 24-hour valet service, spa and fitness center, room service, and an on-site restaurant. Ranging from 800 to 1,500 square feet, the units are much smaller than the regular condos. But they also cost only half as much, from $400,000 to $2.1 million. Hardly a bargain price for most folks, but if you're well off and don't want to spend much time or energy furnishing and managing your unit, a condo-hotel can make sense. Because these kinds of properties are relatively new, it's unclear how well they'll sell in a downturn.

• **Bartering.** Barter adherents like to trade things the old way, before there was money, or even wampum. They simply put a value on whatever they have to offer, from haircutting services to vacation homes, and market it on one of the numerous barter sites on the Web. If someone takes it, the "seller" accumulates points, which can be used to "buy" something another person is marketing.

The upside of this arrangement is, you don't deplete your bank account if you're just trading goods and services. But the downside is, your shopping universe is limited to whatever someone else is bartering.

Still, there are some intriguing possibilities out there. A group of vacation-property owners in Ocean Isle Beach, North Carolina, which markets its units for rent on the Web, is also open to barter. One owner recently advertised that he'd barter a vacation stay for a pool table, kayak, canoe, or small johnboat.

• **Home Swaps.** Catalog-based home exchange networks have been around since the 1950s, but with the advent of the Internet, this rent-free way of exchanging vacation homes all over the world has exploded. It requires a degree of trust, since you'll be sharing your things with complete strangers, and an understanding that the home you get to stay in may not be of the same size and quality as yours— nor will the owners necessarily share your standards of housekeeping.

You also need to come to terms with the people who'll be staying in your home. Who will pay for utilities, maid service, pool cleaning, phone calls, and incidental damage? (Because no money changes hands, insurers usually consider the people who stay in your home as guests, and cover any major damage they may create.) And you'll have to make space in your closets and drawers for the other family's things. Obviously, it makes sense to put all valuables under lock and key. But if you have a sense of adventure and the longing to experience the real comforts of home, rather than an impersonal hotel room or rental cottage, it's worth a try.

Some international agencies have sprung up, both bricks-and-sticks and online, to handle home exchanges for small fees. The benefit of these services is anonymity—you can look over listings before committing, and there's no awkwardness if you decide you really don't want to spend your vacation in a place with plaid wallpaper and a view of the 7-Eleven's parking lot. But you don't necessarily have to join a service to arrange an exchange. One of the best sources for do-it-yourself home swaps is www.craigslist.com, a huge community bulletin board that doesn't charge for listings.

In fact, through a swap I found on Craigslist.com, my next vacation probably will be spent at the lovely home of a California couple in Carmel, or their equally pretty vacation home on Lake Tahoe, while they and their four children stay at my home outside of Washington, D.C. We've even agreed to swap minivans during the stay (as long as our respective teenagers don't drive them).

• **Renting Out Your Primary Home.** If you don't have a vacation home to stay at or swap, you can still underwrite the cost of a vacation home rental or hotel accomodations by renting out part or all of your primary home. Attorney and travel author Elaine Lee converted her two-car garage in her San Francisco Bay–area home into a rental space and used the money to fund a trip around the world. Or, you can subdivide or convert your vacation home into multiple units, living in one and renting out the rest. With luck, you can even make a profit.

- **Mooching.** For the ultimate savings in vacation lodging, brush up on your social skills and wheedle an invitation to be someone's houseguest. It's not as facetious as it sounds. According to the Travel Industry Association of America, that's what 48% of all leisure travelers did last year.

A WORD ON TAXES

With the stroke of a pen in 1997, President Bill Clinton gave homeowners another reason to look at their houses not just as a home, but also as a personal piggy bank.

The Taxpayer Relief Act, signed by the President that year, wiped away the old "rollover replacement rule" that allowed people to defer taxes by rolling over gains into any home they bought or built within 24 months of the first sale. The old law also gave homeowners over the age of 55 a once-in-a-lifetime tax exclusion of $125,000—though you had to be meticulous about keeping records showing any improvements to your home that would raise its cost basis.

The new law is much simpler, and it's not just beneficial to the over-55 crowd. Now, single people can exclude $250,000, and couples $500,000, of increases in their home's value from capital gains (any gains beyond that are taxed at 15%). The only caveat: You must have owned and used the property as your principal residence for two out of the five years prior to the date of sale.

Even better, the law defines "principal residence" broadly. It could be your vacation home, your yacht, even your motor home.

Divorced or separated spouses can use the rule, too, as long as they meet the residency requirements. Only one spouse out

Sharing the Dream Home: The Armendarizes' Story

At age forty, Sheri Armendariz wanted a change. She was tired of working at her family business in Tucson, Arizona, where she'd lived all of her life, and dreamed of owning a house by the sea.

So she drove to San Diego, where she quickly realized that she and her husband Art couldn't afford any of the homes she liked. She kept moving up the coast until she hit Oceanside, California, a community that had once been a beach retreat for silent screen stars like Mary Pickford and Douglas Fairbanks, but which lost its allure for the rich and famous once Camp Pendleton, a Marine base, was built there in the 1940s. To Ms. Armendariz, however, it was "peaceful, without the commercialism, of so many other beach communities."

Ms. Armendariz moved into a hotel and started home-shopping in earnest. "I started looking at apartments and fixer-uppers, but I was so disappointed," she says. "Everything looked so junky." Then, finally, she saw her dream home—a huge home overlooking the ocean.

There were two problems, however: The home was really too big for the couple, who have no children. Plus, the $1.675 million price tag was out of their range.

The couple briefly considered buying the place and operating it as a bed-and-breakfast, but concluded that was too much work. Instead, they convinced a lender to give them enough money to buy the place and renovate it into two separate units, each with kitchen facilities. They stay on one side of the house, which has

(continued)

one bedroom. They rent out the other side, which has three, for $4,000 a week.

It only took a couple of months for the couple to achieve positive cash flow using this method, and rentals remain strong. And they've had another, unexpected bonus—a big equity boost, thanks to rocketing home prices in Oceanside, now one of the hottest vacation home markets in the country. In December 2004, when they refinanced their loan, the home was appraised for $3 million.

of a married couple filing a joint return needs to meet the ownership requirement, though both must meet the residency requirement, to get the full $500,000 deduction. If only one spouse meets both requirements, the exclusion is the same as it would be for a single person.

Although you can only use the exclusion once in a 24-month period, you can get a partial exclusion if you sold the house because you changed your place of employment, had a health problem, or there were other unforeseen circumstances. Under these circumstances, if you and your spouse move because of a job transfer a year after buying a house, you can still exclude up to $125,000 in gains. Also, if you have lived in your home at least a year, but then had to leave it because a health problem required that you stay in a hospital or similar licensed care facility, the time spent in the facility is counted toward the residency requirement.

That's a good way for primary and vacation owners to cut or eliminate their tax bills. Investors have another way. It's called the Internal Revenue Service Section 1031 exchange, also known as a tax-deferred exchange. The exchange requires that you trade an interest that you hold in real estate that you have held for business, trade, or investment reasons for another "like-kind" interest.

The interest can be a sole ownership, tenancy in common, or joint tenancy; the swap can be for any type of real estate other than a primary or secondary residence. For instance, you can trade your rental home for an apartment building, or your shopping center for a building lot. Making a tax-deferred exchange lets you unload a property that is hard to sell or manage, or acquire one with a greater income stream or profit potential.

But to defer all taxes, the replacement property must be of equal or greater value than the property you are exchanging, and you must use all of your accumulated equity to acquire it.

The actual exchange is complicated, and rarely involves an exact one-for-one swap of properties. Instead, it involves a number of players, all of whom are swapping properties with different people, sometimes in different states. And it requires an experienced intermediary (you can find one at most banks or title insurance companies).

The deal works like this: First, after receiving an offer for your property, you assign your rights to the property to the buyer. The buyer gives the intermediary cash, which is put into a trust account that only you can direct. That's the first step of the transaction. Then, within 45 days, you make an offer to acquire replacement property (it doesn't have to be accepted within this time frame). Within 180 days of completing the first step, you must complete the exchange by taking title to the replacement property. You do this by assigning your purchaser's obligations to the intermediary, who acquires the property and tells the seller to deed it directly to you.

However, Uncle Sam frowns on tax-deferred exchanges being used to flip properties, so most accountants recommend that you hold the acquired property for at least six months to a year before you sell.

You can also convert a rental house into a personal residence if you rent it out for some period after you acquire it (although the IRS doesn't specify how long you must do this, most tax advisors recommend at least six months). In October 2004, Congress enacted a new law affecting such a conversion. The law allows you to take the principal residence sale tax exemption of $250,000 for singles or $500,000 for a couple, as long as you hold the property for at least five years before the sale, and occupy it for at least two of those years.

Finally, if you flip properties, the IRS may classify you as a dealer. That's a bummer from a tax standpoint, since dealers can't depreciate any real estate, take advantage of tax-deferred exchanges, or use the "installment" method to report the sale of real estate. Rental income made by dealers is also vulnerable to self-employment income tax. To avoid this, it's a good idea to form a corporation and use it for your short-term purchases and sales.

SURVIVAL TIPS

- **Create a business plan.** Do this before you even think about buying. Figure in expenses, income, maintenance, taxes, depreciation, and how long you plan to own the property. Some good worksheets can be found in *Secure Your Financial Future Investing in Real Estate* by Martin Stone and Spencer Strauss.

- **Research the area thoroughly.** Look at crime rates, the quality of school districts, and local economic indicators (see Chapter 8 for details). If possible, rent a unit in the complex where you want to buy, and see what the neighbors say about it. Especially, check if any special assessments are planned in the near future—for instance, to replace the clubhouse roof or upgrade the golf course.

• **Check homeowner's association rules and local ordinances.** See if there are any rules governing the minimum amount of time that you can rent out your unit, or how often you can rent.

• **Buy in owner-occupied communities.** Try to buy a unit where there are more owners than renters. Properties are generally kept in better condition.

• **Search for granny flats.** Some homes in older communities have "granny flats," or accessory rental units in the backyard. Often, zoning grandfathers these units. If you rent them out along with the main house, you get two-for-one cash flow.

• **Do the commute.** More and more, traffic is figuring in people's minds when they decide where they want to rent, both in primary and vacation home areas. Spend a morning commuting during rush hour to the nearest employment center and the area's most popular attractions. If the commute is short, you can use it in your marketing materials; if it's hellish, you may want to pass on the property.

• **Set ground rules.** If you're buying a vacation home, family and friends may expect to use it for free. If you want to allow this, establish ground rules, especially as to when the unit will be available and who pays for damage and cleaning fees. Otherwise, let everyone know up front that this is primarily an investment for you—though, like the phone company, you may want to offer friends-'n'-family discounts.

• **Check permits.** See how many new units are planned for the area where you plan to buy. Hot markets attract builders, and their units will compete with yours. Most renters prefer new homes to older ones. And the more homes that are available, the lower rents will be.

• **Make sure you have enough insurance.** If you are building a home and acting as your own general contractor, you'll need general liability, builder's risk, and worker's compensation for day laborers not carried under a subcontractor's policy. If you're rehabbing, you'll need to look into insurance against fire and theft. After the work is completed, you'll need insurance for the increased value of the property, with separate riders covering furniture and valuables. Depending on the location, you may also need insurance to protect against floods, hurricanes, or other disasters—assuming you can get it.

• **Inventory the condition of your rental.** When you rent to a tenant, walk through the home together and complete a checklist that inventories the condition of everything in the home, from stains, nicks and chips to the working condition of appliances, windows and doors. Don't forget to write down the paint color and condition of the walls. It's useful to take pictures of every room using a digital camera. Documentation will minimize he said/she said disputes over the condition of the unit when the renter leaves.

• **Understand disclosures.** Know what sort of disclosures you legally need to make to tenants under state and federal laws. Among these disclosures are the existence of lead-based paint or asbestos; illegal controlled substances or carcinogenic materials dumped on the property; and the proximity of a closed military base that housed explosives or ammunition.

• **Be specific about security deposits.** To reduce last-minute misunderstandings with tenants, and avoid possible legal action, make sure your lease agreement specifies whether or not they can use their security deposit to pay their last month's rent when they move.

• **Notify tenants properly before you sell.** If you are selling a house you've rented, make sure you give the tenant proper notification under state law. Typically, tenants on a month-to-month lease can be kicked out if the seller gives 30 or 60 days' notice. Be aware that in many states, you can't make a tenant move out on a weekend or legal holiday, and must extend the notice to cover those days.

SURVIVAL SUMMARY

- Don't buy investment properties unless you're willing to learn what the pros know and will take the time and energy to compete with them.
- When you calculate returns, don't assume properties will appreciate at the same rate they do now. As in stocks, past performance does not guarantee future returns.
- If you're an investor, decide whether you'll be a rehabber, a landlord, or a flipper.
- Look beyond traditional sources of funds to finance your investments.
- Be aware that vacation markets are the most vulnerable to downturns. If the market's peaking, consider other ways to own or use vacation properties.

- Make the most of tax exemptions and deferrals.
- Create a plan and research the neighborhood, the project, and even traffic patterns thoroughly before you buy.
- To avoid disputes with tenants, make sure your agreements with them are clear and in writing.

6

Facing Foreclosure

Back in the 1930s, foreclosures were an unhappy reality that touched nearly everyone. As massive segments of the population lost their jobs, they defaulted on their loan payments. Banks used the foreclosure process, a legal procedure, to gain ownership of the property, which had been pledged as security for the loan. The sheriff came and evicted the weeping owners. Then the banks tried to resell the property, either privately or at auction.

Thankfully, those scenes are much rarer today. It's not surprising, given the hot market that allows people to sell their homes if they get into financial trouble. National foreclosure rates have been falling. During the first quarter of 2005, the rate of loans in foreclosure fell to 1.08%, a decline of seven basis points, according to the Mortgage Bankers Association. The rate of new loans in foreclosure declined slightly, too.

What is surprising is that this happy scenario isn't the case everywhere. In California, the percentage of loans in foreclosure is low at .20%. But in Ohio, it's 3.37%, almost 17 times as high. Jobs, or the lack of them, account for much of the disparity, says Mike Fratantoni, senior director of single-family research and economics for the Mortgage Bankers Association. "Everyone is paying the same interest rate these days," he says. "But local economies matter a lot."

Nevertheless, he's concerned that as more buyers take risky mortgage alternatives like interest-only loans and option ARMs, there will be a rise in foreclosures. That's because most economists expect that the short-term rates used as a benchmark for these loans are headed up (over the past year, one of these benchmarks, the prime rate, went up more than two percentage points). Borrowers who took out ARMs that adjust after six months or a year will be hit, too. "People need to plan for payment shocks," he says.

Of course, you don't need a local economic downturn to fall into foreclosure; bad times can also come should you experience a personal disaster like divorce, illness, or a ruinous legal judgment. The process works like this: If you fall behind as few as three mortgage payments and don't work out a deal, many lenders will initiate a foreclosure proceeding by posting a notice of default or a lawsuit to foreclose in newspaper legal notices and on the Internet. There are ways to forestall the sale, like declaring bankruptcy, or restructuring the note (see below). But then the property goes to auction, where somebody, usually the lender, buys it.

Even that isn't necessarily the end of the story, however, since some places allow original owners or junior lien holders (people who have put a charge against the property for unpaid debts or taxes) to redeem the property for a certain length of time after the sale. If that doesn't happen, the home goes on the lender's books as a "real-estate owned" (REO) property. Specialized brokers market these properties to investors.

Two states, New Hampshire and Connecticut, use "strict foreclosure," which eliminates the auction. Once a court finds the loan is in default, title reverts to the lender. However, borrowers are given a certain grace period in which to redeem the loan.

Although borrowers are given many more chances to avoid losing their properties than they were in the Snidely Whiplash days of the Depression, the experience is still traumatic. Here are some ways for borrowers to stay out of the sort of financial trouble that leads to foreclosures; and for investors, some tips for buying them.

FOR BORROWERS: STAYING SOLVENT

• **Plan for interest rate increases.** The best way to avoid foreclosure is to plan for the worst possible scenario. Experts don't expect this current climate of low interest rates to last forever. So prepare for it, and start saving.

Also, if you took out an interest-only loan or option ARM to get into your house, refinance into something less risky as soon as you can.

And unless you plan to stay in your house only a short time, it's a good idea to use bonuses and other "found money" to start paying down principal (be sure to designate it as such so the lender doesn't count it as prepaid interest).

Over the life of the loan, this will save you big bucks. For instance, if you have a $200,000 30-year fixed-rate loan at 6% on a $240,000 house and pay only $100 extra a month, you'll pay $182,871 in interest over the life of the loan. Without that extra $100 payment, you'll pay $231,676.

• **Review your credit cards.** The average American owes a whopping $8,100 in debts, according to Bankrate.com. Just pay the minimum balance on that debt and incur no other, the company notes, and it will take about 30 years to get rid of the loan.

So cut up all of your credit cards except one or two. But first, determine which ones have the best interest rates, grace periods and late fees, and no or low annual fees. Compare the terms for transferring balances (some card issuers charge a transfer fee, or treat anything other than an initial balance transfer as a cash advance). Make sure any low introductory teaser rates apply to any balances that you transfer, not just initial transferred balances, and make sure the transfer has gone through before you cancel the card. Ask for written confirmation from the credit card company that the card has been canceled, and that no balance, fees, or penalties are outstanding.

Stick the remaining cards under your mattress, in the safe, or beneath those cowboy boots you never wear—anywhere but in your wallet. Vow to go on a strict all-cash diet until you've paid those balances down to nothing.

Once you do, arrange to have your total monthly balance paid automatically out of your checking account each month. You'll have the convenience of using a credit card, but will never get socked with a late fee or a surprise rise in interest rates because you made a late payment.

• **Sell stuff.** This might seen self-evident, but debt counselors say it's amazing how many people travel headlong into foreclosure with two luxury vehicles sitting in their driveways. Selling one used Lexus for $20,000 will buy you ten months or more on the average mortgage. A dining-room furniture set might get you two or three months. That could be just enough time to get a new job and get out of the hole.

• **Talk to your creditors.** If you get in over your head financially, one of the worst things you can do is to stick your head in the sand, especially if you owe more on the house than it's worth. If you do, you may not only lose your house, but also be pursued for the remaining balance through a deficiency judgment.

Instead, make an appointment to visit the lender and bring copies of income statements and any other evidence of why you can't pay. The lender may give you a payment moratorium, work out a repayment plan, refinance the loan, or extend its terms. (Indeed, Fannie Mae and Freddie Mac require their lenders to pursue workouts.)

If you can't repay at all, you may want to sell your house in a preforeclosure sale. Or, you may decide to give the lender a deed in lieu of foreclosure. You wind up with nothing if you do this, but you do preserve your credit rating.

If you are heading for the auction block, ask the lender if he'll give you a lease and an option to buy the property back, should he be the successful bidder. Sometimes lenders will agree, so they don't have to pay marketing or fix-up costs on the house.

• **Consider filing for bankruptcy.** Yes, there's a social stigma and a blemish on your credit record for as long as 10 years when you file for bankruptcy, but it can forestall foreclosure.

Your choices under the Bankruptcy Abuse Prevention and Consumer Protection Act of 2005 are to file under Chapter 7, which allows you to keep some assets and home equity while you sell everything else (the money is split among creditors; most of your other debts are canceled), or under Chapter 13, which allows you to keep more property, including your home, but requires you to file a plan with the court that repays your debt within a three- or five-year period.

State laws govern how much money or property you can keep under homestead exemptions. Some let you keep only a little or no equity on your home. Texas, Florida, Arkansas, Iowa, Kansas, Oklahoma, South Dakota, and Washington, D.C., let you keep all of your equity. State laws prevail in bankruptcy cases filed in state courts.

But a new federal law, passed in April 2005 and effective in October 2005, has toughened many of the old rules of bankruptcy for filings in federal courts. Among its provisions is a rule that prevents people from sheltering their assets by buying a pricey house in a state with liberal homestead exemptions. Unless you've lived in a state for two years, you can't claim the exemption. And unless you've lived in the house, or another in the same state, for 40 months or more, your exemption is now capped at $125,000.

Bankruptcy is a last-resort option, and you shouldn't declare it without talking to a knowledgeable bankruptcy attorney. You can find one through the National Association of Consumer Bankruptcy Attorneys (http://nacba.com) or the American Bankruptcy Institute (www.abiworld.org).

• **Beware of scammers.** When you're desperate, you're vulnerable to people who offer to "rescue" you from your financial difficulties. Such scammers solicit their victims by e-mail, letter or newspaper ads, offering a quick fix for financial difficulties. Some people will offer to take over your mortgage payment while you get back on your feet, or even give you some cash, if you'll deed the property to them. Then they'll rent your house back to you, but not make any mortgage payments. Since you're still responsible for the mortgage, you lose the house and your credit rating is damaged. (A variation on this scam: The "rescuers" have you sign papers that you think are for a new loan, but which actually deed the house over to them.) Others charge high fees for making phone calls to creditors that borrowers could easily do themselves, but don't give any solid help that would keep the house from falling into foreclosure.

The National Consumer Law Center issued a report in June 2005 that talks about rescue scams that are "ripping the homes right out from under thousands and thousands of Americans." In one case, the report describes a seventy-eight-year-old woman who took out a $100,000 mortgage on a paid-up home worth $450,000, then fell behind on payments. A scammer convinced her to sign over the deed to her home in return for a payoff of the mortgage, $3,000, a used Honda Accord, and an additional $5,000 payment when her disabled son died. Then he charged her rent to continue to live in the home. When she finally realized that she'd signed away most of her home's equity, the woman obtained a lawyer, but has yet to recover the deed for the home, where she had lived for five decades. For a copy of the report, visit the center's Web site at www.consumerlaw.org.

FOR INVESTORS: BUYING IN GOOD TIMES AND BAD

Foreclosures happen during booms and busts, but for investors, bad times make for better deals. That's because there are more homes on the market to choose from, and therefore less competition for each home. Currently, there's one foreclosure for every 1,853 households, according to RealtyTrac, a foreclosure data provider, but in some states there are many

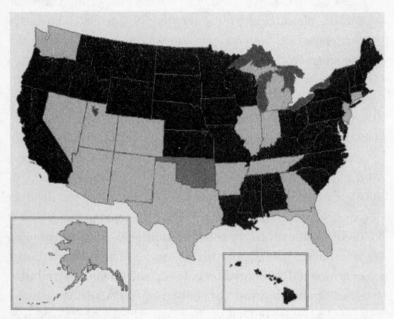

Even in boom times (May 2005), 18 states exceed 110% of the national average rate of foreclosures.

0 to 90% of the National Average = ▪
90 to 110% of the National Average = ▪
> 110% of the National Average = ▪
Note: National Average for May '05 = 1 of 1,854 households
(i.e., ≅ 0.054%) Source: RealtyTrac

more—New Mexico's foreclosure rate is more than three times higher than the average.

Although there are plenty of vultures trying to skim the equity out of homes, most professional foreclosure investors aren't trying to defraud buyers. They're simply using one tool for buying homes at a discount and then reselling them. "The bottom line is, a regular homeowner can afford to pay retail—we can't," says Theron J. Marrs, a foreclosure investor in Vancouver, Washington.

Despite what the late-night real estate hucksters say, not everyone is cut out to be a foreclosure investor. To cut down on competition, many investors generally try to buy houses directly from owners. That, however, can be dicey since sellers are often in emotional distress, embarrassed, and angry that they can't pay their bills—investors tell me they've been harassed, threatened, and even run off the property by tearful owners brandishing shotguns and pistols.

The stereotype of a foreclosure is a house in the slums, but actually, they happen in the same proportion in every neighborhood—there are even multimillion-dollar mansions up for auction. The sorts of problems that cause foreclosure, ranging from divorce to addictions or alcoholism, can happen to anybody.

Most foreclosure homes are in bedraggled condition, however. Homeowners who have gotten to the foreclosure stage have been in financial straits for at least a year or two, and so don't have any money for maintenance, much less niceties. Once they get close to forfeiting their homes, they lose interest even in mowing the grass and getting rid of termites. Moreover, some owners get so angry over the fact that they're about to lose their homes that they sabotage the place—a Las Vegas broker who deals in foreclosures says he's found everything from holes punched in walls to concrete poured down the toilet.

Here are the steps to buying a foreclosure, and some tips:

• **Comb the data.** Data on foreclosure sales can be found by combing through courthouse records, legal newspapers, and legal notices in regular newspapers. Or you can subscribe to Web-based services like Foreclosures.com, Buy-BankHomes.com, ForeclosureNet.net, and RealtyTrac.com.

If you want to buy a foreclosure house listed by the Department of Housing and Urban Development, the Veterans Administration, Fannie Mae or Freddie Mac, you'll have to go through a real estate agent, who'll walk you through technicalities of the sale. Investors will have to put down a hefty down payment, but first-time buyers can sometimes get low- or no-down-payment deals.

• **Meet the owner.** If you are going to get the best deal with the least competition from other investors, you must meet the owner before the house is auctioned. The time period depends on the type of foreclosure proceeding initiated, and whether any defenses are allowed, but usually is about four months after the lender begins the process. That's why professional investors advertise constantly, in newspapers, on street signs, even on magnetic signs attached to their cars.

It's not always possible to visit the property before the sale. But try, because you'll have a better idea of fix-up costs. Some sellers bar buyers from formally inspecting a home before a sale, so this may be the only opportunity you have to determine its condition.

When you meet the owners, see if there is some way to come to terms that will help them with their specific problems—for example, they might need a lump sum of cash to pay off a legal judgment. Listen respectfully, put your offer

in writing, and follow up to make sure the owners understand its terms. After being harassed by lawyers and bom-
barded by offers from bargain hunters, owners are often in
too emotional a state to think clearly.

• **Check out all encumbrances.** A distressed property may be
encumbered by legal judgments, second mortgages, and
other debts, all of which eat up your profits. But you may
not discover them until after the sale. Worse, in some states,
foreclosure sellers are exempted from disclosure laws, so if
you find out that somebody lied to you, too bad for you.

In the preforeclosure stage, when the property still be-
longs to the owner, all of the debts on the property, including
mortgages, mechanic's liens, and unpaid taxes, encumber it.
So if you buy the property, you must pay off these debts. You
must also find all of the owners on the title, and get them to
sign off on the sale. Anyone who has put a charge or lien on
a property and hasn't been paid can initiate the foreclosure
process. Usually, that's the lender who has put the first mortgage on the property, known as the first lien holder. (Liens
are considered senior or junior depending on the order in
which they were recorded, not the amount owed.)

At auction, the first lien holder (usually the bank) can
wipe out all other liens if he's the successful bidder. But the
first lien holder isn't always the one foreclosing. So if you
win the auction, you can inherit problems clouding the title.
Also, in some cases, junior lien holders or the original owner
can redeem foreclosed properties after the sale by buying
out the first lien holder's position; you get nothing, in that
case, except the interest rate on the note over the redemption period. (Indeed, some foreclosure investors just skip
the auction and try to control property after the redemption

period by buying junior liens or title from the original owner.) A title search can determine which lien holder is foreclosing. Always write your contracts "subject to title report," so you can back out of the deal if the property is too encumbered.

• **Hold the line on price.** Most investors don't like to bid at auctions, and in fact, about eight out of 10 homes that go to the courthouse steps are bought back by the lender.

There are many downsides to buying at auction—you have to make the decision quickly on little information, you usually have to come up with cash on the spot, and you may have to evict tenants or owners if you're the winning bidder.

But you can make money on courthouse-step deals, seasoned investors say, if you pay no more than 75% of the property's market value. The trick is to know the true market value, which you should determine in advance through recent comparable sales, and as much presale on-site sleuthing as you can arrange.

• **Check out the REOs.** Once the lender takes back the property as an REO (real-estate-owned) property, you'll likely get a better deal than you would on the courthouse steps. That's because once the lender has the loan back on its books, it faces holding and management costs, real estate agent commissions, and possibly costs to upgrade the property. REOs can be found through the REO departments of banks, though many lenders prefer to sell through local brokers who specialize in this work.

You may have a hard time getting the bank to give you financing on the loan, however. Banks generally want foreclosures off their books, and they don't want to be associated with them in any form.

Buying from the Bank:
Alfred Murciano's Story

Six years ago, pediatrician Alfred Murciano was looking for foreclosed properties in Coral Gables, Florida, when he stumbled on a neglected mansion.

The owner had paid more than $1 million for the property, but had defaulted on the loan. The bank foreclosed, and now wanted $890,000 for it.

The house, which sat on an acre of ground, had a good layout and was basically livable, but had peeling paint, an old kitchen, and outdated appliances. Dr. Murciano negotiated a price of $540,000 with the bank, which gave him an interest-only loan for 70% of the purchase price, then spent $100,000 out of pocket fixing the place up, even adding a swimming pool.

It was a lot of work, but when Dr. Murciano sold the house recently, he made $500,000. "As an investment," he says, "the value was there."

SURVIVAL SUMMARY

- Expect mortgage interest rates to rise over the next few years, and plan your finances accordingly.
- Figure out what you'd need to survive in the event of job loss or illness of at least six months, and save enough to tide you over.
- Eliminate most credit cards, and transfer balances to the ones with the lowest interest rates.

- If you get in financial trouble, talk to your lender before it's too late.
- File for bankruptcy as a last resort.
- Beware of people who want to "rescue" you from financial woes by taking over your house.
- Consider investing in foreclosures only if you have the time to investigate encumbrances, title, and the condition of the house.
- To get the best deals, buy foreclosures before or after the auction.

7

Going Global

 While we Americans have been having a Maalox moment worrying about housing bubbles, the rest of the world has been watching—and buying anyway.

Given how weak the dollar has been against major currencies over the past few years—and how expensive homes are abroad—it's no surprise foreigners consider our homes terrific deals. Until the dollar dramatically strengthens, expect these trends to continue. George Ralph Lilley, an Englishman who runs an international luxury-car-repair business, owns a house in Denver and is looking to buy two more somewhere in the Rockies—a ski condo for his own use, and one for his company's employees. "Everybody I know in London is looking for a place in America," he says. "Who minds a little jet lag?"

Brokers say that most are visitors looking for pieds-à-terre, investment properties, and vacation getaways. Fortunately for us, foreigners are most interested in buying in resort and coastal areas—the very places most vulnerable to price declines. Every seller in a frothy market should be thinking of ways to grab their attention.

After all, they have the buying power. Since 2002, the British pound has risen some 35% against the dollar. Meanwhile, over the same period, the Canadian dollar rose 30%, the euro 50%, the Australian dollar 40%, and the yen 22%. Unless the dollar rallies substantially, this built-in discount will continue to make our homes attractive to buyers from overseas, even when our fellow Americans have gone back to investing in bonds instead of bungalows.

And compared with many places in the world today, America is a luxurious bargain. In Tokyo, the most expensive city in the world, the average apartment is only 775 square feet, compared with the average New York apartment of 1,334 square feet. German single-family homes cost about the same as their American counterparts, but are only about half the size. In France, a Parisian flat with a newly renovated kitchen might have only a single sink and a two-burner stove, while a country farmhouse is sure to have peeling paint and primitive plumbing.

Also, because of deregulation, Internet buying, price wars, and new players in the airline industry, as of this writing international flights remain very reasonable. As long as round-trip tickets from Madrid to Chicago, or New York to London, can be had for around $400, as they currently can, the United States will be very inviting.

Political, legal, and economic turmoil has been sending foreigners to our shores, too. Russians have been buying property in the United States to move money out of an unstable economy; one New York broker brags that he's sold $18 million worth of real estate to Russian buyers in the past few months. The French look to America to avoid their country's restrictive inheritance laws, which require up to 75% of an estate to be left to close relatives like parents, spouses, or children; the English, to escape high property taxes.

The creation of the euro six years ago also has worked to our advantage. Before, Germans who wanted to buy a villa somewhere along Spain's Gold Coast could wait for favorable exchange rates. They can't play that sort of currency game in Europe now, so they look to Florida's Gulf Coast instead.

And some foreign buyers are beating out Americans when it comes to buying new homes in preconstruction phases, when they're often the cheapest—for instance, a British businessman recently bought a two-bedroom apartment in a new Manhattan high-rise for $1.1 million, one day after it hit the market.

Larry Cheshire, a salesman for Fox and Jacobs Homes in Dallas, says foreign demand for American homes is so high, some buyers are purchasing them sight unseen and asking for samples of paint chips and rug swatches to be shipped overseas. The buyers move in without ever seeing the house or meeting a customer service representative face-to-face. "They see American homes as unbeatable investments," he says.

For all the appeal that American properties have to foreigners, however, it's still a big world. How do you attract attention, navigate financial and cultural problems, and finalize the deal? And conversely, if you find the American housing scene has become too expensive, how can you still find bargains abroad?

FOR SELLERS

Spreading the Word

THE INTERNET

The Internet has become a global bazaar, the place most people look first to check out goods and compare prices. For home shoppers, it's especially popular. You can check out neighbor-hoods without having to spend any money on gas or airline tick-ets, or peek into someone's kitchen and bedroom using virtual tours without having to endure an agent's pushy prattle.

If you've listed your house with a real estate agent, it's likely that your house will be listed on the Web, on the company's Web site, and also on the granddaddy Web site of them all, Realtor.com, the official site of the National Association of Re-altors, run by a Westlake Village, California–based company called HomeStore. The site boasts some 2 million listings, and can be accessed by anyone in the world. It also links to a site called Worldproperties.com, the International Consortium of Real Estate Associations' Web site, which boasts 3 million list-ings in 20 countries.

But be aware that American megasites have some limita-tions for foreigners, because they're geared toward people who already understand how our system works. Australian Andrew Brooke, who owns an animal training business and is looking to buy a place in Las Vegas, complains that American real estate Web sites don't have enough information on establishing credit with U.S. banks, or on how Americans price their homes. "We Australians just love to negotiate," he says.

There are some ways to get additional exposure, if you're willing to shell out a little money on your own. Many Web sites visited by foreigners primarily for purposes other than home shopping have begun to include real estate listings. Compared with the big real estate sites, the pickings are puny, but that does mean your ad will stand out.

For instance, Cyberrentals.com shows vacation rental prop-erties worldwide, but also has an international section of homes for sale. Early this summer, its listings ranged from a one-bedroom, $90,000 Vermont cabin to a compound of three cottages overlooking Nantucket Sound for $1.5 million. Listings cost $75 for three months. Thirty dollars buys an ad for a month on Escapeartist.com, a site popular with those looking for international jobs and relocation information; recent listings include everything from a 250-acre Indiana horse farm for $690,000 to a $3.99 million Florida mansion with a private dock for a 175-foot yacht. Graeme Glade advertised on this site because he felt his $3.75 million home on the north shore of Oahu was too expensive to appeal to local buyers, and received inquiries from Asia and Europe, plus an offer from an Englishman. "How better to market your home when you're 3,000 miles from the nearest continent?" he says.

Of course, thanks to software like Front Page or DreamWeaver, building your own Web site isn't that difficult anymore. Some home sellers spend $450 or more to buy software to translate their sites into foreign languages, but it really isn't necessary. Popular search engines like Google now automatically translate pages into dozens of languages, including Bulgarian, Xhosa, and Zulu.

Ken Knowles, who owns an electronics company, taught himself how to put up his own Web site so he could market his $1.2 million Auburn, Kentucky, mansion, complete with helicopter landing pad. It brought him a lot of attention—he had at least 4,000 hits and a few offers. But he also had to sift through a lot of Nigerian scam letters (one man offered to buy his house if he'd just send along his bank account and Social Security number), phony offers, and outrageous demands. "One even asked me to supply a caretaker and some servants," he said.

PRINT

Obviously, you can always buy an ad in a big international newspaper. But if you have a home in a place that's likely to appeal to a particular nationality or ethnic group, then it also makes sense to advertise in local papers that appeal to them. For instance, because Cape Coral, Florida, has a sizable German population, one builder there advertises heavily not only in German newspapers and Lufthansa flight magazines, but also in local German-American club publications, on the theory that recent immigrants keep up ties with friends and relatives in their homeland.

Brokers also suggest advertising in publications that don't have a real estate focus, but are likely to be read by foreigners. Publications aimed at doctors, lawyers, and other professionals, who are more apt to have high disposable income, are particularly good. Other choices to explore are publications focusing on hobbies or recreational passions, like golfing, boating, or fishing. Alumni magazines are another frequently overlooked source, and they often hang around a long time on coffee tables. A classified ad in *Oxford Today*, which is published only three times a year to correspond to the British academic year, costs two pounds (roughly $3.80) a word.

If your house is posh and you want to make a splash, you might also want to advertise in a glossy listing magazine that reaches an international audience, like *Unique Homes*. The homes featured in this publication are pricey, averaging $2 million to $3 million, and so are the ads, which cost around $3,500 a page (a Web ad is included). But the publication reaches 80 countries around the world. Thomas DuPont, publisher of the St. Petersburg, Florida–based *DuPont Registry of Homes*, says demand by foreign distributors for their luxury magazine is up 12% in 2005 over 2004, and they're selling especially well in international airports. Ads in the magazine cost about $2,500 a page, and include an Internet ad.

Making Connections

Let's face it: We're a nation of gossipers. So if you list your home with a real estate agent in America, just about every other real estate agent in the country can find out the details through multiple listing services. Real estate agents routinely refer clients to other agents across town or even across the country for a small fee.

But outside of the United States, most countries don't have multiple listing services or agents that cooperate. In fact, in many countries, real estate agents are unlicensed and may have other jobs, like truck driving or hairdressing. Buyers often have to go from one agent to another to see all the homes for sale in an area, since agents only show their own listings. San Francisco real estate broker Olivia Hsu Decker, who often deals with foreign brokers and buyers, says, "Even in Europe, it's still very backward."

Though some brokers are starting to invite American brokers to their trade shows, their main networking events, on the whole brokers are suspicious of each other and unwilling to share information.

But American brokers are trying to go global. According to the National Association of Realtors, about half of all agents say they have done at least one international transaction. The trade group reports that some 39,000 agents say international deals are the primary or secondary focus of their business, an increase of 56% since 2001.

It pays to look for agents who are looking to advance their education in international deals. Over 1,000 agents have taken training to become "Certified International Property Specialists," which requires them to take a seven-day course that looks into such issues as taxes, regional market conditions, currency exchange rates, and cross-cultural relationships. After getting this certification, some agents take another three days of courses focusing on issues surrounding corporate relocation to become "Global Mobility Specialists." More than 400 agents worldwide have this certification. To encourage agents to cooperate more across borders, last year the International Network, an arm of the National Association of Realtors, launched the Transnational Referral Certificate program—registering any agent worldwide who passes a six-hour online exam in the network's database, which the agents can access. If you want to sell abroad, make sure that your agent has this certification, since foreign agents in the program will be more likely to trust them.

Big real estate franchisors are trying to widen their global presence. Re/Max, the Greenwood Village, Colorado, company, has been expanding rapidly, and now has more than 100,000 agents worldwide and offices in 54 countries, including Cyprus, Wales, and Zambia. France and the Czech Republic were signed up just since the beginning of 2005. Century 21, a Parsippany, New Jersey–based real estate brokerage with franchises in 43 countries, has expanded its foreign offices by 17% over the past year, to 3,060. This year, it plans to roll out a "lead router" that in a matter of seconds connects a foreign buyer who expresses an interest in an American property listed on the company's Web site with a United States–based agent who speaks his language. "We're trying to break down all the obstacles," says Tom Kunz, the company's chief executive officer.

Luxury property brokerages like Christie's Great Estates are expanding abroad, as well. The Sante Fe, New Mexico–based company has offices in 19 countries, mostly in Europe, and plans to move into South America and Asia soon. The company prints and distributes about 4,000 copies of its thick listing magazine abroad, and keeps one-page brochures of listings in its auction houses in Geneva and Hong Kong. The downsides: Though there are no lower limits on home prices the company will handle, the average price is $5 million. And forget it if you live in states like Alaska, North Dakota, or Nebraska, where the company has no offices. "We concentrate on the most affluent areas," says company president and chief executive officer Kay Coughlin.

Show Me the Money

Sellers often snap up offers by foreigners for the very same reason that buyers hate to compete with them in bidding wars: Foreigners usually pay cash.

That's because it's difficult for foreign buyers to get financing here. Their credit information isn't tracked by the three big agencies that keep track of Americans' bill-paying habits; so banks can't just pull up their FICO scores to see if they'd be a good candidate for a loan (for more on FICO scores, see Chapter 2).

Instead, they have to prove to American banks they're creditworthy by providing proof they've paid their bills on time, as well as proof of income. Banks have to verify this information, often through unfamiliar channels. The process can take months. Although some big international banks like Credit Suisse and Barclays will make loans on overseas purchases, and a few specialize in it, like British-based Conti Financial Services, most lenders just don't want to be bothered. Those that do typically require big down payments of 20% or more.

Unless they take out loans in their native currency, foreign buyers also have to worry about movements in exchange rates that don't work in their favor. To minimize risk, some are buying forward time option contracts that fix the rate of exchange. For instance, Foreign Currency Direct, a firm based in Buckinghamshire, England, guarantees exchange rates for two years.

It's all such a hassle, many foreign buyers just decide to refinance their primary homes and use the equity to buy here, or turn to relatives for financing. In some cultures, particularly Hispanic and Asian ones, groups of friends and family pool money for home purchases in informal banks. Sometimes they want to check out the investment before lending the money, so don't be surprised if a large group shows up to check out your house.

Seller financing will make your home more attractive to foreign buyers, especially if you can offer a rate just below what lenders are asking. Have an attorney draft the contract, and include a provision that the money will be drawn automatically from the buyer's account and deposited in yours. Make sure you're paid in dollars, though as an added incentive, you could offer to adjust payments to a lower rate in case the dollar rises against the buyer's currency.

Sealing the Deal

When an American sells to another American, everybody knows the rules of the game. But when you sell to a foreign buyer, both of you probably are in for some culture shock.

For starters, even in English-speaking countries, the process is very different than it is here. In this country, homes that go to auction are usually distressed properties or in foreclosure, but in Australia, it's a common way for homes to be sold. Moreover, each Australian state has its own real-estate licensing law, and not all of them require agents to be tested.

Meanwhile, in England, buyers often find homes just by walking around a neighborhood that interests them looking for for-sale signs. Owners and sellers often negotiate directly, and agents, if they are used at all, sometimes do little more than handle the paperwork. Deals take weeks or months to cement, and can fall through at any time, even at the closing table.

This means that many foreigners have had more direct experience in negotiating real estate deals than most Americans, who leave the mano-a-mano wrangling to their agents. Agents say that the typical deal in the United States involves an offer that's perhaps 10% or 20% below the asking price, with two or three rounds of counteroffers. But foreigners may offer about half of the asking price and go up by slow increments, refusing to split the difference and patiently trying to wear down the seller's resistance. "Americans get insulted," says Olivia Hsu Decker, the San Francisco broker. "They don't realize that this is how people in other parts of the world bargain."

Moreover, the expectations that each side brings to the deal about how and when negotiations should proceed are often at odds. Some buyers, especially in Asian and South American countries, won't finalize a purchase until the elders in the family approve it. In India, real estate brokers continue to negotiate their rates with clients even after a deal is done. Many buyers continue to haggle long after the contract is signed. One California agent who sold a $9 million home says the Filipino buyer demanded all of the home's furnishings and the seller's sports car on the day of settlement—and kept pushing until he got them.

If you're selling your home without the help of an agent, keep in mind that verbal promises are taken more seriously in many other parts of the world than they are here. Your word may be considered your bond. In South Korea, deals are often consummated with a handshake, and long written contracts are regarded with suspicion; in Saudi Arabia, oral contracts are enforceable if witnessed.

On the other hand, because they aren't familiar with our system, expect foreign buyers to look more carefully at every aspect of the deal. Brian Chadbourne recently bought a newly constructed home in Mill Valley, California, for $4.5 million, and insisted on having all the inspections and surveys redone—even though the seller, a builder, will be his next-door neighbor. It's a matter of habit, not trust, he says, since in his native England, buyers frequently bring in their own set of experts to verify information. "You can't rely on thirdhand advice," he says.

Taxes

If you sell a house to a foreigner, especially without the help of a real estate agent, you should be aware of the tax rules that govern the sale.

Since 2003, the Internal Revenue Service has required all foreigners who either buy or sell a real property interest in the United States to have Individual Taxpayer Identification Numbers. It's not a simple procedure, requires proof of identity such as a passport, driver's license and/or birth certificate, and a copy of the sales contract, and can take up to six weeks. So sellers who require a quick closing should make sure that this vital piece of information has been obtained, or at least is in the pipeline.

If the foreigner plans to rent out the home he's buying from you, ask if he's consulted a good international tax attorney or certified public accountant. There's a thicket of complicated rules governing rental income and withholding and estate taxes, and you don't want your buyer backing out of the deal at the last minute when he realizes just what's involved.

For instance, foreigners can choose to pay taxes at a flat rate of 30% (some countries have treaties with the United States to prevent double taxation), but then may not deduct expenses for utilities, maintenance, or mortgage interest. The tenant must withhold the tax from the rent and remit it to the IRS.

Or they can choose to have the income taxed as "effectively connected U.S. source income," which does allow for deductions, provided that the property is rented for more than 15 days.

Depreciation is allowed, deducted as an expense from income, but is recaptured when the property is sold. Foreigners also get hammered on estate taxes, though again, treaties preventing double taxation may soften the blow.

FOR BUYERS

Getting a Bargain Abroad

The weaker the dollar gets against most of the world's currencies, the dimmer my fantasy becomes of owning my own mango farm in the tropics. But there are places where Americans can still come out ahead, either because our dollar still has some muscle against the native currency, or because things are simply cheap there—or both. Although there are some caveats, here are some places where you can still find bargains (for more, visit Escapeartist.com).

CROATIA

Since the Balkan conflict ended a decade ago, Croatia, with more than 1,000 miles of coastline along the Adriatic Sea, has been rediscovered. Last summer when our cruise ship stopped in Dubrovnik, famous for its red-tiled roofs and massive city walls, the city was so overrun with tourists, we had a hard time navigating the narrow, medieval streets.

Ferry boats run often to resort towns and islands along the coast. Although you'll pay a premium to buy in euros, at this writing, prices are still relatively cheap. In Cavtat, a village about fifteen minutes from Dubrovnik, a new one-bedroom apartment with views of the bay and mountains sells for 81,000 euros ($104,016). A three-bedroom apartment in Dubrovnik was recently listed for sale for 300,000 euros ($385,191); an 18th-century castle with 7,300 square feet for 650,000 euros ($834,582). In many places, prices have more than doubled in the last three years.

Be sure to get a competent agent and legal advice before buying in Croatia, however. Since the Balkan war caused massive emigration, titles aren't always clear. Homes are frequently in need of massive renovation, and access to the property may be poor. Be sure to specify everything you want in the sale, including the lot itself. Also, check to make sure that utilities are available. In some places, you may have trouble getting a septic tank permit.

Expect to pay 5% of the purchase price for property tax, and 1% in legal fees. If you sell within three years of purchase, you'll owe a capital gains tax of 35% of the profit (no capital gains tax is owed if you keep the property for longer than three years). If you rent out the house, you must pay 25% of the profit on this income.

DOMINICAN REPUBLIC

Only $29,000 buys a one-bedroom condo, while $165,000 gets a three-bedroom villa in the beachfront town of Sosua. But you have to be a risk taker to live here: Over the last two years, the U.S. embassy reports, crimes ranging from pickpocketing to home invasions have been on the rise here. Moreover, overworked registrars often tell buyers that a home title is clear when it isn't.

Nevertheless, restrictions on foreign land ownership have been lifted in recent years, and property taxes are very low. You can also keep the interest earned on any U.S. dollars banked in the country, tax-free.

Taxes and expenses are about 5% of the purchase price. Some attorneys will suggest that you record a lower purchase price to lower the transfer tax, but don't be tempted. Once you sell, you're subject to the Dominican Republic's 25% capital gains tax.

Should you die, the law requires that you reserve part of your estate for certain heirs like children, whether or not you've written a will stating otherwise—unless you hold your property through a holding company. Inheritance taxes range from 17% to 32%, depending on the relationship between the deceased and the heir. If the beneficiary lives outside of the Dominican Republic, there's a 50% surcharge.

PANAMA

Since the Panamanian balboa exchanges one-for-one with the U.S. dollar, you don't have to play any currency games here. A 20-acre coffee plantation was recently advertised for sale at $312,000. (Blame the collapse of world coffee prices, despite the inroads that Starbucks has made into every hamlet in America.) Inflation is low, and so is the cost of living. Restaurants and groceries cost about half what they do stateside.

Although there is still some lingering resentment of Americans, who occupied the Canal Zone for 93 years (our troops pulled out on the last day of 2000), the occupation did allow the country to build up its banking system. And it's one of the safest places south of the United States border.

If you're 18 (yes, even that young) or older and qualify for a pension of $500 or more from any source ($600 for a couple), you can get discounts for half off on closing costs, and more. You also don't have to pay property taxes for 20 years if you buy or build a new house.

But you need to check ownership history carefully. Sometimes squatters claim properties through "right of possession." Should you buy one of these and the rightful owner appear, you'd have to give it up, although the claimant would have to reimburse you for the purchase price.

PHILIPPINES

In a country made up of 7,000 islands, there are lots of bargains, especially in the more remote areas. In Los Banos, a house with four apartments, each with three bedrooms, is on the market for $160,000. In Puerto Princesa City, Palawan, a thatched bayfront house on stilts is for sale, along with all the furniture, two outrigger boats, and two motorcycles, for $29,500 (property taxes are $12 a year).

As in Thailand and Indonesia, there are complex rules governing what and how much foreigners can own. Foreigners cannot own land in the Philippines. Former Filipinos can, if they haven't given up their rights to citizenship. But there are restrictions on how big a property former Filipinos can purchase, and foreign spouses and children can't inherit it. To get around these rules, you need to form a corporation with a Filipino partner, or get a special retirement/investment visa, which requires that you be at least 35 years old and meet bank deposit requirements.

Non-Filipinos can own up to 40% of a condo complex, however, and these units can be passed on to anyone. Developers in these towers often provide financing, but beware of the terms, since they are often for five years with double-digit interest

Purchasing a Philippine Paradise: The Littles' Story

Lots of people dream about owning an exotic island in a different country, but Dick Little and his wife actually did it.

The Littles are both American citizens, but Mrs. Little was born in the Philippines. Almost six years ago, they learned that one of her distant relatives was interested in selling her a Philippine island that she owned called San Dian. The couple, who then lived in San Diego where Mr. Little had recently retired from his job as a university professor, went to investigate.

They stayed for three months in a one-room hut with no facilities, "but with the unsurpassed beauty of the place all around us," Mr. Little recalls. To their delight, they discovered the island had 60 coconut trees, a coral reef, a sandy beach, and no mosquitoes. They returned to San Diego, rented out their house, and went back to San Dian.

But the process of buying a place in the Philippines is complicated for a foreigner. Even though Mrs. Little is a native Filipino, the fact that she is an American citizen made her subject to the country's rule that foreigners cannot own land. Instead, they had to find a native Filipino to act as a "trustee" to become the titular (legal) owner of the property.

The Littles found a bank manager in a city near their island who acted as their trustee. "The trustee has no rights regarding the property," says Mr. Little. "He cannot buy, sell, or rent it, nor prevent the actual owner from doing what he wants with it. The trustee cannot even set foot on the property without the owners' permission."

(continued)

Over the next two years, they built two houses on the island, and installed everything that was needed to bring the island into the modern age, including a solar electric power system, satellite television and telephone, an electric winch to move their speedboat out of the water, toilets, two septic tanks, and water tanks that collect rainwater. To be completely self-sufficient, they also put in pens for chickens, turkeys, and pigs.

But living on the island had its drawbacks. They were 20 miles by sea from the nearest town, which limited grocery shopping to weekly trips and outside entertainment to a monthly trip to Cebu, which was an overnight boat trip. As their daughter, who was born in the Philippines, neared school age, they reluctantly decided that the time had come to leave. "The educational system in the Philippines is woefully inadequate," Mr. Little says, "so we had no choice but to move back to the States."

Though a 3.7-acre oceanfront property with two houses anywhere in the United States would be gobbled up in a heartbeat at the Littles' $250,000 asking price, they've had it for sale on three different Web sites for several months with no takers. Part of the problem may be suspicion of the trustee system, enacted to prevent foreign owners from grabbing all the best land. "There has long been talk of opening up land to foreign residents and investors, but things move pretty slowly in the Philippines," Mr. Little says.

rates. Foreign owners can also rent out their properties, but don't expect too much—the Philippines has some of the lowest rents in Asia.

Unlike the United States, who pays the taxes is negotiable. Usually, sellers pay the 6% capital gains tax, the 1.5% document stamp tax and other lesser taxes and fees, but sometimes buyers are pressured to pay them. New homes have a hefty 10% capital gains tax, but occasionally this tax is included in the sales price as an incentive.

THAILAND

Since the end of 2004, the country has been devastated by a tsunami, a major earthquake, and a series of terrorist bomb blasts. But surprisingly, the real estate market has remained resilient. Real estate agents say they have had more than a few bargain hunters, but prices have softened only a little. Since the disasters, a Hong Kong investor purchased a villa for 99 million bat ($2.5 million) in the resort city of Phuket.

In the past decade, Thailand's real estate values have increased tenfold, but the cost of living is still cheap. Beachfront land starts at about $200,000; a compound of four houses in Nai Harn Beach overlooking rice paddies with buffaloes was recently advertised on the Internet for $230,000.

As in the Philippines, there's a catch: Foreigners can't own land in their own names. Instead, they have to make 30-year-lease deals with holding companies or other local owners and these can be legally questionable. Also, keep in mind that the Thai real estate industry is unregulated. Use a broker who's a member of the Thai Real Estate Broker Association, who will have an identification card.

SURVIVAL TIPS: BEFORE YOU BUY ABROAD

• **Secure financing before you start searching.** Foreign lenders will likely charge much higher interest rates than you can get here. In Argentina, for instance, interest rates can be as high as 18%. Most lenders will demand a hefty down payment of at least 20%, but may require as much as

70%. Loan periods in other countries are often shorter, typically 20 years, but may be as short as five years.

• **Specify everything you want to convey in the sale.** In countries like France, sellers routinely take everything with them, including the appliances and even the kitchen cabinets.

• **Check out closing costs.** Buyers in the United States are used to paying no more than 6% to close a deal, but you may have to pay much more in other countries, including value-added and other taxes, and registration and legal fees. For example, in France, closing costs can be as much as 10% of the purchase price. Also, in the United States, sellers usually wind up footing the bill for both the buyer's and the seller's agents; in other countries, buyers may be asked to split the bill.

• **Hire your own attorney.** In other countries, closings are often handled by notaries or other officials who have no obligation to look out for your interests.

• **Beware of leaseholds about to expire.** A property sold as a "freehold" allows for perpetual ownership, but some properties are sold as "leaseholds," which end after a certain time period and can be renewed or cancelled at the landlord's discretion. This may not matter if you're at the beginning of the leasehold, which typically lasts for 99 years, but it loses value considerably toward the end. For instance, a fabulous 2,800-square-foot apartment with gold-leaf ceilings in London is currently on the market for £1.6 million, but its leasehold expires in 2014; meanwhile, a smaller, less glamorous place nearby with a freehold tenure is selling for £2.85 million. Lenders generally won't finance a place with less than 75 years left on the lease.

• **Look into insurance against catastrophes.** With the tragic tsunami in Asia, 2004 was the most expensive year in modern times for natural disasters, with $105 billion in property damage. According to the U.S. Geological Survey, there are more than 3 million earthquakes worldwide each year, with about 900 measuring 5.0 or higher on the Richter Scale. Eight out of 10 occur in Pacific Rim countries. It is difficult to get insurance against such catastrophes, but some places like Japan do offer government-reinsured earthquake and typhoon insurance, though premiums can run as high as 10% of the price of the house, and deductibles of 50% or more.

• **Supervise remodeling in person.** Practically speaking, you often have to act as your own general contractor in other countries, and you are responsible if there are any accidents on the property. An American who bought a home in Mexico had to pay $8,000 to correct mistakes when workers put walls and windows in the wrong places.

• **Check for hidden costs before you do improvements.** In some countries, like Mexico, you may have to pay workers' Social Security taxes.

SURVIVAL SUMMARY

If you want to sell your home to foreigners . . .
- Advertise in journals foreign buyers are likely to see, including trade, professional, and alumni publications.
- Since foreigners are likely to see your home on the Internet first, advertise on several Web sites, and make your own Web site, if possible.
- Look for brokers who are Certified International Property Specialists.
- Remember that financing is difficult for foreigners to obtain, so seller financing is a good incentive.

- Be sensitive to cultural differences that can ruin a deal. Especially, don't be insulted if a seller's opening bid for your home is low.

If you want to buy a bargain home abroad . . .

- Look beyond the usual tourist spots to less-visited places. But pay attention to regulations that restrict ownership and inheritance.
- Check out taxes and settlement costs. Don't assume that customs about who pays what are the same as they are in the United States.
- Understand that foreign interest rates and terms are likely to be higher than they are here, so pay cash if possible.
- Keep in mind that real estate agents and others involved in real estate deals may not be licensed or trained, and may not be looking out for your best interests. Hire your own attorney.
- Remember that verbal agreements and handshakes are considered binding in many parts of the world.
- Be aware that there may be restrictions as to what kind of property can be owned by foreigners. Some property may also be sold as leaseholds that expire after a certain period.
- Get a title search and check chains of ownership carefully.
- Get insurance against catastrophes like earthquakes and tsunamis, if you can.
- Supervise any fix-up work in person, and find out who's liable if there's an accident on your property.

8

Catching the Next Wave

In Grandma's day, kids vied to control Atlantic City's real estate sitting around the *Monopoly* board. Today, they buy buildings playing *Donald Trump's Real Estate Tycoon* on their mobile telephones.

It seems the real estate fantasy never dies.

Once you grow up and real money enters the picture, however, the decisions stop being fun and become stomach churning. You know you must buy low and sell high to win the game, but how do you know where you are in the real estate cycle? Even the experts aren't completely sure. "You don't really know if you're in a bubble until it's over," says Thomas Lawler, senior vice president of risk policy at Fannie Mae.

So all you can do is to look at the economic tea leaves. At this writing, interest rates remain low, but the Federal Reserve is continuing its attempts to curb the "irrational exuberance" of the real estate markets.

Home prices have been clambering upward at a dizzying pace, but there are signs of cooling. The Commerce Department's most recent report at this writing, in May 2005, shows that the median sales price of new single-family homes has dropped 6.5% from the month before, to $217,000. That's the lowest level that prices have been since September 2004. The median new-home price peaked in February 2005 at $237,300.

Some high-flying markets are already showing some signs of coming down to earth: Leonard Steinberg, senior vice president of Prudential Douglas Elliman, a major New York brokerage, says he's seeing an increase in the length of time properties are on the market, more broker incentives, and some price reductions, as well as deals falling through because of "jitters" and "second thoughts."

And still people buy—despite the warnings and the daily drumbeat of news stories warning of bursting bubbles. Indeed, according to the latest figures from the National Association of Realtors, existing-home sales in May 2005 were up 3.5% over the year before; new-home sales for the same month were up 4.4% over the prior year, according to the National Association of Home Builders.

In more than twenty-five years of writing about real estate, I've gone through several complete housing cycles, and I've noticed a curious phenomenon. No matter how sophisticated, educated, and experienced my sources are, it's almost impossible for them not to get caught up in a herd mentality. When prices are heading down, experts talk about how bad times are here to stay; when they're on the upswing, they explain away any signs that the market is weakening.

But if there is anything I have learned, it's that nothing lasts forever, neither the good times nor the bad. And though the trick to thriving is absurdly simple—just figure out where in the

Is the Price Right?

For both buyers and sellers, price is the main focus of any real estate deal. It's more than just a number; it's an ego validation. Buyers want to brag that they got a bargain. Sellers want to say they sold for top dollar. Neither side wants anyone to think they were poor negotiators, or sold at the wrong time, or let the other side get the upper hand in the deal.

That's why everyone turns a hawk's eye on national average and median home prices and appreciation rates, even though these are abstractions that have nothing to do with what's happening on the only place that really matters, on your street. Psychologically, we need benchmarks to compare our success, relative to the "norm"—even though there is no norm.

We use "comparable" home sales to help us figure out how to price out homes, even though these are pretty sorry tools. A four-bedroom house on a half-acre lot in a neighborhood a mile from your house could be pretty similar to yours, or worlds apart, in a buyer's eyes. And yet, the typical way that real estate agents help you come up with a listing price is to get nearby home sales for the previous six months that are about the same size and age as your place, average them, and then add a little extra to cover the commission and some "haggling room."

Armed with the same data from their real estate agents or Web searching, buyers make their offers. This meeting of the minds is far less scientific than sellers, buyers, or their respective agents pretend it is. Homes aren't commodities like stocks, bonds, or cars; even when new, they've been customized, decorated, and cared for. They symbolize the personalities of the people who've

(continued)

created them. That's why, whether we're buying or selling, emotions play a greater role than they do in just about any other purchase we make.

So we can't tell you how to price your home. All we can do is suggest that you, like everyone else, arm yourself with recent "comps." Then, if the market is stable, add between 5% and 10%, which is the usual discount that buyers demand.

You'll know your market is stable if homes are appreciating near their historic norms (you'll have to find out the local rate yourself, but for the past decade, they've run between 4% and 6% nationally).

As cycles move toward their peaks and troughs, however, prices will be much harder to set. Oddly enough, at both points in the cycle, agents say, sellers are more likely to overprice their homes than they are in normal times. At the peak, sellers are influenced by greed, trying to get a better price out of panicky buyers than the neighbors. At the bottom of the cycle, they're motivated by fear, worried that some bottom-feeder will take advantage of them.

But at both the top and the bottom of the cycle, many agents say it makes more sense than usual to price your house *under* the market, perhaps as much as 10%. Though counterintuitive, underpricing "creates excitement," according to Montclair, New Jersey, real estate agent Roberta Baldwin. In a down market, underpricing conveys the fact that a seller is serious, which will attract buyers while the listing is freshest and easiest to sell. But in a hot market, when most houses are overpriced, an underpriced house stands out even more. Ms. Baldwin says that in her town, a home priced below market at $995,000 recently sold for $1.3 million as buyers fought to buy it, while a similar one priced slightly above the market at $1.2 million is still for sale.

cycle you are—you need to be familiar with some economic measures besides the obvious one, home prices, to get a handle on it. Since all of these measures matter to greater or lesser degree depending on the prevailing economic winds, I've put them in alphabetical order:

- **Appreciation.** Appreciation is simply a measure of how much your home has changed in value over the prior 12 months. Economists determine the rate of appreciation by looking at actual changes of home prices over time. In real estate, appreciation can be positive (increase in value) or negative (decrease in value).

    From this, they report the "nominal" rate of appreciation, which is the observed change in value. This is the number you read about in the newspaper when you hear home prices rose nationally at a certain rate.

    But inflation alters those gains or losses. So economists also figure the "real" rate of appreciation, which is the nominal rate minus the rate of inflation. This is a more realistic measure of what your home is worth.

    Over the last five years, nominal price appreciation was 6.5%, and real price appreciation was 3.8%. That's a good return for homeowners, especially compared with the unleveraged returns of other investments like stocks and bonds. But it's also unusually high. Throughout the 1990s, appreciation was much more sluggish, with nominal appreciation averaging 3.75%, and real appreciation at 1.28%. In the late 1980s and early '90s, homes overall actually lost value in real terms, down 4.4% in 1989, 2.5% in 1990, and .4% in 1992.

    The Office of Federal Housing Enterprise Oversight issues a quarterly report of home price trends down to the metro level at www.ofheo.gov. The site also has a calculator that you can use to help establish the current estimated market value of your home.

• **Employment.** Economists obsess over this indicator, and so should you. The reason is obvious: Without jobs, few can afford housing. David Berson, chief economist at Fannie Mae, says, "We have never seen significant price weakness without a decline in job growth and a weakening economy."

National employment figures are worth watching, but more as an indication of where the economy is heading and consumer confidence—people are less inclined to buy not only if they've lost their jobs, but if they're worried about losing them. Employment and unemployment figures for national, state, and metro areas, plus information on mass layoffs, can be found on the Bureau of Labor Statistics Web site, www.bls.gov.

But government statistics lag reality, so read the business section of your newspaper to find out what local companies are planning in terms of hiring and firing, expansions and relocations. If a big local employer is public, keep track of its profits—a sharp decline could mean pink slips for workers in your town.

• **Gross Domestic Product Growth.** Gross domestic product, also known as GDP, is the inflation-adjusted total value of the country's production over the period of a year. It includes the purchases of domestically produced goods and services by people, businesses, foreigners, and the government. You can find this number at the Bureau of Economic Analysis at www.bea.doc.gov.

GDP is important because it shows whether or not the

overall economy is growing at a healthy rate. Dave Seiders, chief economist for the National Association of Home Builders, expects GDP growth to hover in the 3.2% to 3.3% range over the next year, which he calls "not overly exuberant."

• **Housing Affordability Index.** This index, put out by the National Association of Realtors, measures whether or not a buyer earning the nation's median income can qualify for a mortgage on a median-priced, existing single-family home, assuming a 20% down payment.

The higher the index rises, the more affordable homes are. In other words, if the index is 130, the typical family has 130% of the income necessary to buy the home; if it's 100, the family has just enough income; if it's lower than 100, the home is out of reach, at least by conventional lending standards. Higher mortgage rates and home prices can both erode a buyer's purchasing power.

Although based on national figures, buyers still have more than enough income to make the purchase, but rising home prices are making it more difficult. In April 2005, the index reached 122.3, the lowest level in two years. The index is published on NAR's Web site, www.realtor.org.

• **Household Formation.** As people create new living units through marriage, divorce, birth, or "in-migration" (moving to town), naturally, they need shelter. Projections on the 2000 U.S. Census suggest household growth will be strong over the next few years, with 1.5 million to 2 million more people than previously anticipated. David Lereah, chief economist for the National Association of Realtors, projects that over the next decade, demand from new households will reach 16 million to 20 million, while the supply of homes, in the 15 million to 18 million range, won't keep up. Census statistics are available at www.census.gov.

• **Interest Rates.** How much house you can buy, and how cheaply a builder can deliver it to you, all depend on the cost of borrowing. And though local booms and busts can happen independently of the direction of interest rates, in general, housing is sensitive to their swings.

The fate of long-term interest rates is dependent on global forces. At this writing, they remain near historic lows (though most economists do expect them to increase in the coming years).

But short-term rates are much more directly influenced by the actions of the Federal Reserve. Indexes that the Fed controls, like the federal funds rate (the interest rate on overnight loans between banks), and the federal discount rate (the rate at which banks can borrow funds directly from the Fed), have both increased over the last year, and more bump-ups are expected.

The prime rate, which is the lowest commercial interest rate that banks charge to their most creditworthy customers and moves in lockstep with the federal funds rate, has increased more than 2 percentage points over the last year. Now at 6.25%, housing economists expect the prime rate to reach 7% by the end of 2005, and perhaps rise by another quarter of a percentage point next year. Other short-term borrowing benchmarks are also currently on the rise, including the one-year Treasury, the six-month London Interbank Office Rate (LIBOR), the 12-Month Treasury Average (12 MTA), and the 11th District Cost of Funds Index (COFI). This affects consumers who have an adjustable mortgage tied to the prime, of course, but it also impacts other aspects of the home-owning equation. Most builders and materials suppliers borrow money at rates tied to the prime rate or the six-month LIBOR. As their borrowing costs increase, so will the prices of new homes.

Long-term interest rates, which set fixed-rate mortgages, are sensitive to swings in the bond market, and many economists are worried that the two-decade-old bull bond market is ripe for decline.

Interest rates are widely reported, and can be easily found on the Web. A good source for finding comparative rates for your city is www.bankrate.com.

• **Investors.** When too many investors enter the market, watch out. Nationwide, the number of investors in the market is alarming, economists say, accounting for about a quarter of all homes sold; in stable times, the number is closer to 6%. During the first four months of 2005, investors accounted for nearly 10% of the mortgages used to buy homes in the United States, compared to 6% in 2001, according to LoanPerformance, a unit of First American Corp. that tracks mortgage data.

Some economists believe the actual number of investors may be lower than reported. Lenders typically charge people who plan to rent their homes higher interest rates to mitigate the wear-and-tear rentals receive and the higher risk of default. So many borrowers lie about their intentions on their loan applications, since legally, there's little risk of penalty—they can always say they changed their minds about renting after the closing. So unfortunately, while knowing the number of investors in your community is important, it's difficult to find reliable data.

However, you should still talk to local lenders, real estate brokers, homeowner association presidents, and others to get a sense if the number of investors is increasing in the area where you want to live. Should your real estate market start to tumble, investors will be the first to cut and run, and you may find yourself living in a ghost town.

• **Materials Costs.** What builders pay for materials, like lumber, gypsum, steel, and cement, directly affects what you'll have to pay for a new home. With the record numbers of homes under construction in boom markets around the country, many materials are in short supply. Nor is this just a domestic issue, since countries all over the world are experiencing their own building booms and are competing fiercely for these resources. China especially was a major competitor in 2004, leading to spot shortages of some materials in this country.

Every month, the U.S. Bureau of Labor Statistics releases monthly producer price indexes of materials and components for construction, including such materials as softwood lumber, steel mill products, plywood, building paper and board, concrete, and gypsum. For more information, go to www.bls.gov/ppi.

• **Mortgage Applications.** The Mortgage Bankers Association releases a survey of mortgage activity each week that measures the lending activity of a representative sample of the largest mortgage companies in the country. One index produced by this survey, the purchase index, measures the amount of activity from people who are borrowing to buy homes. Economists use this number as a leading indicator of future home sales. An index number greater than 300 suggests a strong market, while one below 200 suggests a weakening one. The index is published on the Web site www.mbaa.org.

• **Pending Sales.** In March 2005, the National Association of Realtors released a new indicator of housing activity called the pending sales index. It measures signed contracts for existing single-family homes, condos, and co-ops. (Signed contracts are not counted as sales until the transaction closes.) Unlike sales data, which shows only what's happened in the past, this index shows what sort of activity can be expected in the near future, one or two months in advance. To follow the index, go to www.realtor.org.

• **Permits.** Permits show an intention by a builder to construct a home, apartment, or other type of real estate. Unlike starts, which show you what's already happened, permits are a leading indicator. Their biggest drawback, in terms of their crystal-ball value, is that not all permits become houses—when markets start to cool, builders simply don't act on the permits they've taken out.

Along with starts, sales, and supply, this statistic gives you an idea what new-home builders have planned for your market. If permits start to fall, it's a sign that builders are pulling back. Permit data can be tracked on the National Association of Home Builders' Web site (www.nahb.org) or on the U.S. Census Web site (www.census.gov).

• **Pre-Sales.** There's no good way for a consumer to track this information statistically, but if you read in your daily newspaper that local home builders are reporting campouts or waiting lists, it's a given that your market is on the upswing. It also may be a sign that the market is close to its peak, since this sort of mania becomes more frenzied as flippers start "turning" contracts before builders get their certificates of occupancy (see Chapter 5 on Investing).

• **Starts.** The U.S. Census Bureau issues figures on the groundbreaking of new homes every month; you can get local figures from your local home building association. Along with permits, sales, and inventory levels (supply), starts give you an idea of whether your area is becoming overbuilt, which can cause prices of all homes to drop. You can find the information at www.census.gov or at the Web site of the National Association of Home Builders, www.nahb.org.

• **Sales.** Closed sales are an obvious indicator of the health of your market, but unlike pending sales, they are a lagging indicator. Data on new- and existing-home sales on national, state, and metropolitan levels can be found on the Web sites of the U.S. Census (www.census.gov), the National Association of Realtors (www.realtor.org), and the National Association of Home Builders (www.nahb.org). However, local real estate agents or data providers may have this information on a county or Zip code level as well.

• **Supply.** Supply is one of the major factors influencing the direction of home prices. According to the National Association of Realtors, inventory reached a record low in the first quarter of 2005 of 4.2 months' supply. Equilibrium is 6 months' supply, the organization says. But when inventory reaches 9 months, as it did during the 1990–91 recession, sellers beware—it has become a buyers' market. Inventory levels can be found on www.realtor.org.

Because of the lessons they learned during the last big downturn, builders are fine-tuning the supply of new homes much more than they were doing in the past. Then, builders would buy land, create a subdivision of 100 or more homes, and sell them. Now builders are more likely to option land from the owner, build a small model complex, and build homes only as they're sold.

Of course, by controlling the supply, builders are also more able to control prices than in the past. If homes are selling well, builders can bump up prices to match demand; if they aren't, they run "close-out" specials.

What throws builders off their game are local construction labor shortages, shortages and price run-ups for land and materials, and an influx of investors who buy homes and flip them before the builder has closed out the project.

Dave Seiders, chief economist for the National Association of Home Builders, says that despite these problems, builders should be able to keep up their current pace of building about two million units a year over the coming decade.

However, local markets are always vulnerable to fluctuations when a big builder leaves, no-growth advocates are elected to county councils, or other similar constraints arise. Your local building or real estate brokers association can give you insight into housing inventory levels in your area.

• **Time on the Market.** In boom times, homes may be sold within hours of reaching the market, but as markets cool, they linger. How long a home sits on the market is one of the first signs of cooling, in fact, since it usually takes a while for sellers to realize the market has turned and to drop their prices.

In 2004, the typical home stayed on the market for four weeks, according to the National Association of Realtors. But this is a statistic that really only matters on a local level; check with your local brokers association.

EPILOGUE

In a career spent writing about real estate, I've heard homes referred to in many ways, from "the Money Pit" to "the Ultimate Money Machine." But by far, the most common cliché that gets bandied about is "the American Dream."

It seems to me that the dream has been expanded of late, far beyond ballooning home prices. Homes are no longer just our shelter, our nest eggs, and our refuge from the outside world. They've become the symbols of our self-worth, our net worth, and our status. And they've become our prime investments: our college funds, our pension funds, our cash cows, and our financial chess pieces.

Homes, the government and the real estate industry have decided, are places we should own, not rent, no matter how shaky our credit or how big a financial risk we must take to get them. Homes, real estate speculators tell us, are things we shouldn't consume but collect. Homes are not homes at all, but the salvation for us as individuals who forgot to save for retirement, and also for us as a society that has lost so much of its economic punch to a falling dollar, a huge deficit, and increasingly muscular global competitors.

That's an awful lot of weight to put on a vinyl-sided tract house. And if we listen to these voices, when the cycle turns, as it inevitably will, we'll feel our disappointment in more than our wallets. We'll feel like fools for encasing our hopes and financial futures in bricks and sticks. We'll feel trapped by the physical embodiment of dashed dreams. We'll feel house poor.

Some perspective is in order. Our home's address isn't Easy Street. It's simply a place to live, and a solid investment over time—if we can afford it, don't overpay, make smart improvements, and don't get caught up in risky financing schemes.

So my parting advice is to think of your house as your grandparents did—as the setting for your life's triumphs and intimacies, fights and fantasies, heartbreak and memories. And when you finally leave it, let it be because it's the right time to go, not because you're worried the market will boom or bust.

Let your home be the place where you dream the American Dream—but not the dream itself.

SOURCES AND RESOURCES

Agence France Presse

American Bankruptcy Institute (www.abiworld.org)

American Farmland Trust (www.farmland.org)

AnnualCreditReport.com (www.annualcreditreport.com)

Assist-2-Sell (www.assist2sell.com)

The Australian

Bankrate.com (www.bankrate.com)

Barclays (www.barclays.com)

Barron's

Bob Bruss Real Estate Center (www.bobbruss.com)

Bronchik, William. *Financing Secrets of a Millionaire Real
Estate Investor.* Chicago: Dearborn, 2003.

Bronchik, William, and Robert Dahlstrom. *Flipping Properties.*
Chicago: Dearborn, 2001.

BUILDER

BuyBankHomes.com (www.buybankhomes.com)

Census Bureau, U.S. (www.census.gov)

Center for Economic Policy Research (www.cepr.net)

Christie's Great Estates (www.christiesgreatestates.com)

Commerce, Department of (www.commerce.gov)

Consumers Union (www.consumersunion.org)

Conti Financial Services (www.mortgagesoverseas.com)

Corcoran Group (www.corcoran.com)

Craigslist.com (www.craigslist.com)

Credit Suisse (www.credit-suisse.com)

Cyberrentals.com (www.cyberrentals.com)

DataQuick Information Systems (www.dataquick.com)

Decker Bullock (www.deckerbullock.com)

DeCima, Jay. *Start Small, Profit Big in Real Estate.* New York: McGraw-Hill, 2005.

Debtsettlementusa.com (www.debtsettlementusa.com)

Domainia.com (www.domainia.com)

DuPont Registry of Homes

East West Mortgage (www.ewmortgage.com)

Economic Analysis, Bureau of (www.bea.doc.gov)

Economy.com (www.economy.com)

Edelman, Ric. *The Truth about Money.* New York: Harper, 1998.

Eldred, Gary. *Beginner's Guide to Real Estate Investing.* New York: Wiley, 2004.

———. *The 106 Common Mistakes Homebuyers Make (And How to Avoid Them).* New York: Wiley, 2002.

Energy, Department of (www.energy.gov)

Equifax (www.equifax.com)

Escapeartist.com (www.escapeartist.com)

Experian (www.experian.com)

Faber, Marc. *Tomorrow's Gold.* Hong Kong: CLSA Ltd., 2002.

Fair Isaac Corporation (www.myfico.com)

Fannie Mae (www.fanniemae.com)

Federal Deposit Insurance Corporation (www.fdic.gov)

Federal Housing Enterprise Oversight, Office of (www.ofheo.gov)

Federal Reserve (www.federalreserve.gov)

FISERV/CSW (www.cswv.com)

Forbes

Foreclosures.com (www.foreclosures.com)

ForeclosureNet.net (www.foreclosurenet.net)

Foreign Currency Direct (www.currencies.co.uk)

ForSaleByOwner.com Corp (www.forsalebyowner.com)

Fortune

Fox and Jacobs Homes (www.centexhomes.com/FoxAndJacobsAbout.asp)

FreddieMac (www.freddiemac.com)

Fremont Bank (www.fremontbank.com)

FSBO.com (www.fsbo.com)

Galbraith, John Kenneth. *A Short History of Financial Euphoria.* Knoxville: Whittle Direct Books, 1990.

Garton-Good, Julie. *Real Estate A La Carte.* Chicago: Dearborn, 2001.

Glink, Ilyce. *100 Questions Every First-Time Home Buyer Should Ask.* New York: Three Rivers Press, 2005.

The Globe and Mail

Goldman Sachs (www.gs.com)

Guttentag, Jack. *The Mortgage Encyclopedia.* New York: McGraw-Hill, 2004.

Heavens, Alan J. *What No One Ever Tells You about Renovating Your Home.* Chicago: Dearborn, 2005.

HedgeStreet Inc. (www.hedgestreet.com)

Help-U-Sell (www.helpusell.com)

Hill, Robert J. *What No One Ever Tells You about Investing in Real Estate.* Chicago: Dearborn, 2005.

HMS National (www.hmsnet.com)

Holbert, Hugh, and Ron Tepper. *The Real Estate Investor's Q and A Book.* New York: Wiley, 1992.

Homeownership Alliance (www.homeownershipalliance.com)

Home Warranty of America (www.hwahomewarranty.com)

Housing and Urban Development, Department of (www.hud.gov)

Housing Market Report (www.marketresearch.com)

Inman News Service (www.inman.com)

Inrealty (www.inrealty.com)

Internal Revenue Service (www.irs.gov)

International Monetary Fund (www.imf.org)

Ipsos U.S. Express (www.ipsos-insight.com)

Irwin, Robert. *Find It, Buy It, Fix It: The Insider's Guide to Fixer-Uppers.* 2nd ed. Chicago: Dearborn, 2000.

John Burns Real Estate Consulting Inc. (www.realestateconsulting.com)

Joint Center for Housing Studies (www.ichs.harvard.edu)

Journal of Real Estate Research (www.aresnet.org)

J. P. Morgan Chase and Company (www.jpmorganchase.com)

Kelly, Tom, and John Tuccillo. *How a Second Home Can Be Your Best Investment.* New York: McGraw-Hill, 2004.

Kiplinger's Personal Finance

Labor Statistics, Bureau of (www.bls.gov)

Lank, Edith, and Dena Amoruso. *The Homeseller's Kit.* Chicago: Dearborn, 2001.

Lending Tree (www.lendingtree.com)

Lereah, David. *Are You Missing the Real Estate Boom?* New York: Doubleday, 2005.

Levine, Mark Lee. *International Real Estate.* Chicago: Dearborn, 2004.

Levitt, Steven D., and Stephen J. Dubner. *Freakonomics.* New York: William Morrow, 2005.

LoanPerformance (www.firstamres.com/products/
    loanperformance.jsp)

Los Angeles Times

Marshall and Swift (www.marshallswift.com)

Martindalecenter.com (www.martindalecenter.com)

McCabe Research (www.mccaberesearch.com)

Miller, Peter G. *The Common-Sense Mortgage*. Chicago:
    Contemporary Books, 1999.

Money

Mortgage Bankers Association (www.mba.org)

Myers, Kevin C. *Buy It, Fix It, Sell It, Profit*. Chicago:
    Dearborn, 2003.

National Association of Consumer Bankruptcy Attorneys
    (http://nacba.com)

National Association of Exclusive Buyer Agents
    (www.naeba.org)

National Association of Home Builders (www.nahb.org)

National Association of Real Estate Investment Trusts
    (www.nareit.com)

National Association of Realtors
    (www.realtors.org; www.realtors.com)

National Consumer Law Center (www.consumerlaw.org)

National Real Estate Investors Association
    (www.nationalreia.com)

Newsweek

New York Times

Oregonian

Orman, Suze. *The Road to Wealth*. New York: Riverhead Books,
    2001.

Owners Advantage LLC (www.owners.com)

Oxford Today (www.oxfordtoday.ox.ac.uk)

Park Avenue Mortgage Group (www.parkavenuemortgage.com)

Pivar, William H. *Real Estate Investing from A to Z.* New York: McGraw-Hill, 2004.

Prudential Douglas Elliman (www.prudentialelliman.com)

Real Estate Journal.com (www.realestatejournal.com)

Realtybid.com (www.realtybid.com)

RealtyTrac.com (www.realtytrac.com)

Reed, John T. *Real Estate Investor's Monthly* (www.johntreed.com/realestate.html)

Re/Max (www.remax.com)

Remodeling

Restore Media LLC (www.restoremedia.com)

Schumacher, David T., and Erik Page Bucy. *The Buy and Hold Real Estate Strategy.* New York: Wiley, 1992.

Shell, G. Richard. *Bargaining for Advantage: Negotiation Strategies for Reasonable People.* New York: Viking Press/Penguin Books, 1999.

Shiller, Robert J. *Irrational Exuberance.* Princeton: Princeton University Press, 2005.

Silvercrest Western Home Corporation (www.silvercrest.com)

Smart Money

SRI Consulting Business Intelligence (www.sric-bi.com)

Stone, Martin, and Spencer Strauss. *Secure Your Financial Future Investing in Real Estate.* Chicago: Dearborn, 2003.

St. Petersburg Times

Time

Total Protect (www.totalprotect.com)

TransUnion (www.transunion.com)

UCLA Anderson Forecast (www.uclaforecast.com)

Unique Homes

Wall Street Journal

Washington Post

WCI Communities (http://wci.wcicommunities.com)

Whitney, Russ. *Millionaire Real Estate Mentor.* Chicago: Dearborn, 2003.

Yankelovich Inc. (www.yankelovich.com)

Ziprealty (www.ziprealty.com)

INDEX